12.95

/

M

GREAT MYSTERIES

Stonehenge

OPPOSING VIEWPOINTS®

Look for these and other exciting *Great Mysteries: Opposing Viewpoints* books:

GREAT MYSTERIES

Stonehenge

OPPOSING VIEWPOINTS®

by Peter and Connie Roop

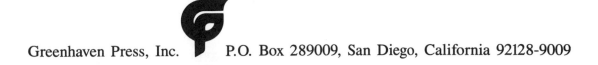

Greenhaven Press, Inc.　　P.O. Box 289009, San Diego, California 92128-9009

Library of Congress Cataloging-in-Publication Data

Roop, Peter.
    Stonehenge : opposing viewpoints / by Peter & Connie Roop.
        p.   cm. — (Great mysteries)
    Includes bibliographical references.
    Summary: Presents opposing viewpoints on the origin and purpose of the mysterious megalithic monument in England.
    ISBN 0-89908-066-9
    1. Stonehenge (England)—Juvenile literature. 2. Wiltshire (England)—Antiquities—Juvenile literature. 3. Megalithic monuments—England—Wiltshire— Juvenile literature. [1. Stonehenge (England) 2. Megalithic monuments. 3. England—Antiquities.] I. Roop, Connie. II. Title.   III. Series: Great mysteries (Saint Paul, Minn.)
DA142.R66   1989
936.2—dc20   89-37441
                                                          CIP
                                                          AC

"When men and women lose the sense of mystery, life will prove to be a gray and dreary business, only with difficulty to be endured."

Harold T. Wilkins, author of Strange Mysteries of Time and Space

Contents

Introduction

This book is written for the curious—those who want to explore the mysteries that are everywhere. To be human is to be constantly surrounded by wonderment. How do birds fly? Are ghosts real? Can animals and people communicate? Was King Arthur a real person or a myth? Why did Amelia Earhart disappear? Did history really happen the way we think it did? Where did the world come from? Where is it going?

Great Mysteries: Opposing Viewpoints books are intended to offer the reader an opportunity to explore some of the many mysteries that both trouble and intrigue us. For the span of each book, we want the reader to feel that he or she is a scientist investigating the extinction of the dinosaurs, an archaeologist searching for clues to the origin of the great Egyptian pyramids, a psychic detective testing the existence of ESP.

One thing all mysteries have in common is that there is no ready answer. Often there are *many* answers but none on which even the majority of authorities agrees. *Great Mysteries: Opposing Viewpoints* books introduce the intriguing views of the experts, allowing the reader to participate in their explorations, their theories, and their disagreements as they try to explain the mysteries of our world.

But most readers won't want to stop here. These *Great Mysteries: Opposing Viewpoints* aim to stimulate the reader's curiosity. Although truth is often impossible to discover, the search is fascinating. It is up to the reader to examine the evidence, to decide whether the answer is there—or to explore further.

''Penetrating so many secrets, we cease to believe in the unknowable. But there it sits nevertheless, calmly licking its chops.''

H.L. Mencken, American essayist

One

What Is Stonehenge?

Imagine it is four thousand years ago. Men, women, and children walk silently outside the ring of standing stones. They have come from the isolated tribes scattered throughout the fields and forests of southern England. They are gathered to worship this one sunrise, the sunrise celebrating the life-giving light of summer. Friends and family, many who have not seen each other for a year, hold hands as they surround the stone ring, making a circle around the holy shrine. One more year has passed, one more cycle of seasons, one more round of the eternal dance of the sun.

The warm wind whips across the wide plains. The green of early summer lies gently upon the land as the damp winds sweep over the hills and valleys.

Sunrise today marks the midpoint of the season when the sun reigns triumphant. The small fields of barley are growing tall, the children running free over the warm earth.

All faces turn to the east, eagerly awaiting the rising of the sun, the bringer of light, the bringer of warmth.

Silence reigns inside the circle of giant stones. The circle of priests, mirroring the circle of people, faces east, too. Their eyes focus on the point directly over the Sunrise Stone, the tall rock marking the rising of the sun on the longest day of summer, the solstice.

A reconstruction of Stonehenge as it may have appeared in the final phase of construction. Did people come here to worship the sunrise?

This is the one time all year when the sun stands for a moment above the stone.

Yet everyone wonders, what if the great ball of the sun did not stop momentarily over the Sunrise Stone? What if the mighty sun did not pause and then roll forward? Would disaster track the tribes, bringing their doom?

Each year the people wondered and worried what would happen if the sun should roll backward off the Sunrise Stone? Yet each year since the giant stone circles had been built, the sun had fulfilled its promise to the people. It rolled forward, leading them into another year.

Suddenly, it happened. The gray sky in the east gave way to the spreading gold of the rising sun. Even the wind seemed to grow still as the golden rim of the sun slipped into the sky, its first thin sliver appearing directly over the Sunrise Stone. The sun seemed to stop, suspended, then climbed higher and higher. Simultaneously, a shout rose from the priests and the people.

The sun, almighty sun, had blessed the people for another year.

Right: Stonehenge just after dawn on midsummer. Opposite page: The small inset map shows the area of England where Stonehenge is located. The larger map gives more detail of the Stonehenge area. Marlborough Downs, near the top of the map, and Old Sarum, near the bottom, are two locations referred to in this book.

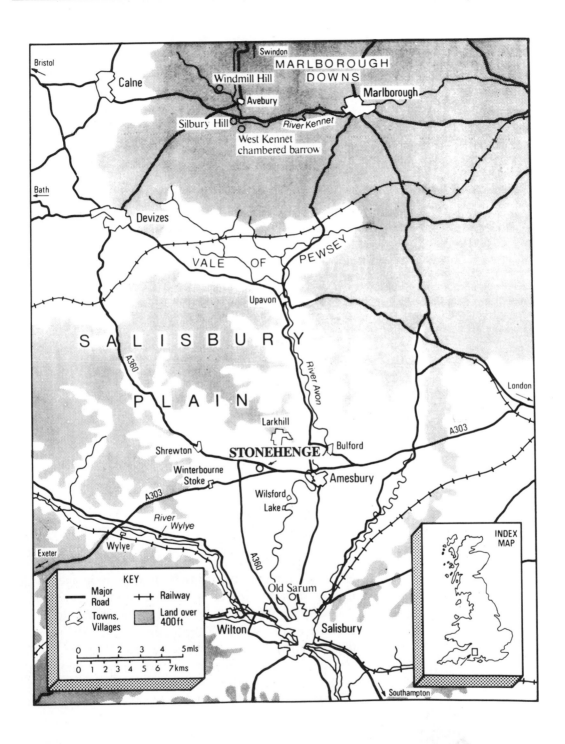

Above: Stonehenge's magical ring is visible from miles away. Opposite page: This map shows the distribution in the British Isles and northern Europe of stone circles, stone alignments (rows and designs), and stone and wood burial chambers. These ancient monuments all have various similarities in appearance and construction to Stonehenge.

This is one scenario, one imaginative guess, about a summer sunrise at Stonehenge many centuries ago.

But was the sun really worshipped at Stonehenge? Many people, scientists and lay people alike, disagree about sun worship at Stonehenge. Even today we do not know the real purpose of this awesome monument. Tall, stark, looming against the sky in an open field, Stonehenge invites us to explore its mysteries and to try to discover its secrets. Since it was built thirty-five hundred years ago, the massive monument has continued to perplex and puzzle millions of people.

A Unique Monument

Stonehenge is unique among the monuments of the ancient world. Isolated on a windswept plain in southern England, built by a people who left no written records, Stonehenge challenges our imaginations. Who was the creative mind behind Stonehenge? Was this mysterious ring of stones a religious center or a seat of kingly power? Was it a gigantic calendar or a guide to the stars? Where were its gigantic stones quarried and how were they moved? Why are there no other monuments quite like Stonehenge among the ancient stone structures scattered throughout Europe?

No one knows the answers to all of these questions.

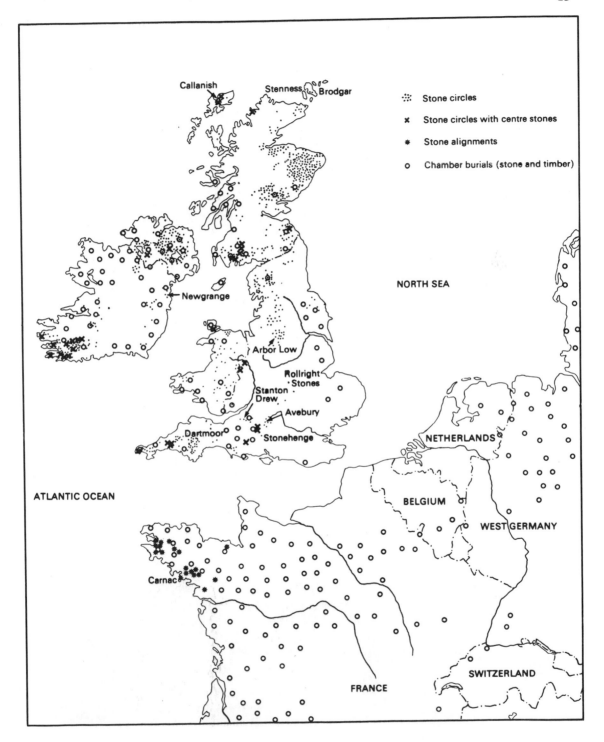

There are many possibilities, many theories, and many opposing views about the mysteries of Stonehenge.

The stones themselves stand silent, brooding, almost daring us to try to discover their secrets. Over the centuries some of their secrets have been revealed, but many more mysteries remain unsolved.

Where Is Stonehenge?

In comparison to other ancient stone monuments such as the Pyramids, Stonehenge is tiny. It is barely thirty-five paces across and could easily fit under the dome of the Library of Congress. Stonehenge would be dwarfed in a modern football stadium.

The impressive stone circle stands near the top of a gently sloping hill on the Salisbury Plain, about thirty miles from the English Channel and eighty miles west of London. The ring of stones is visible over the rolling hills for a mile or two in every direction. Although Stonehenge is perched alone on the hill, the surrounding area has many other prehistoric earthworks, burial mounds, and stone rings.

Stonehenge is one of over fifty thousand prehistoric "megaliths" (Greek for "great stones") in Europe. As a ring of stones, it is by no means

Stonehenge has been marred by people through the centuries. At various times in recent years, protesters and others have painted grafitti on the ancient stones.

In an effort to protect Stonehenge from the wear and tear of the millions of tourists who visit it each year, the British government has enacted various laws. Today there are only certain times when people are allowed to roam freely through the stone circle. Most of the time tourists are kept at a safe distance by fences and guards.

unusual. Dozens of stone rings are scattered around Great Britain alone. Yet because of its unusual size and construction and its mysterious purpose, Stonehenge is unique.

As Stonehenge is approached, the forty giant stones seem to rise from the earth to touch the sky. Most of the stones stand twenty-four or more feet high, four times taller than a tall person. Some weigh as much as forty tons. Others are smaller, weighing only five tons. At first glance the stones may seem to be a natural formation. But a closer look shows that only human imagination and determination could have created Stonehenge.

Time and Deterioration

The Stonehenge of today looks quite different from the Stonehenge of old. Wind and weather have destroyed a little of Stonehenge over the ages. People have destroyed much more. Today less than half of the original stones still stand as their builders planned. Many of the once upright stones lie on their sides like resting giants. Religious fanatics who felt threatened by the mysteries posed by Stonehenge knocked over

A diagram of Stonehenge. The labeled parts are often mentioned in this book. Note, for example, the Avenue, the Aubrey Holes, the Altar Stone, and the Heel Stone.

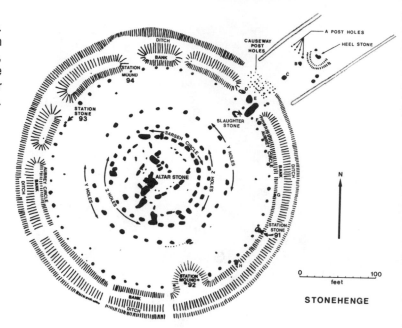

STONEHENGE

many of the standing stones. They pulled them down in an effort to destroy the mysterious monument. They toppled some of the huge stones which then split into pieces. They buried others. Other stones were "quarried" over the centuries as free building material and hauled away for fences, houses, and barns. Even into this century visitors have come to see Stonehenge armed with hammers to carry a chip or chunk away with them to use as a paperweight or doorstop.

Damaged from Sightseers

Only in recent years has the great stone monument been protected from the ravages of people. No longer can one roam among the stones, rubbing hands over the cool giants. Too much damage, intentional or not, has been done by the hundreds of thousands of annual visitors. Today's tourists are even prevented from walking between the stones for fear that their millions of footsteps each year would make the towering rocks unstable.

Stonehenge has a number of major components.

Foremost is the towering stone rings aligned to face northeast/southwest. There are also stones standing alone, a circle of small pits around the large rings of stones, two rings of earth and a ditch surrounding the entire structure, and a wide avenue that approaches the monument. All of these elements are united in the overall design of Stonehenge, clearly indicating that the ancient builders left nothing to chance and that each component had its own purpose.

Stonehenge was not built by one group of people. We know this because there are three major portions of the monument that differ from one another. Differing styles and construction materials reflect the three hundred years of building that took place at Stonehenge.

Three hundred years would be about ten generations of builders. While that may seem like a long time for any community of people to be committed to one building project, during the Middle Ages (2,500 years after Stonehenge was completed), whole families, from great-grandparent to great-grandchild, labored for over a hundred years to build a single cathedral.

How Did the Ancients View Stonehenge?

To better understand Stonehenge and its mysteries, we must first picture Stonehenge as the ancients saw it after the entire structure was completed.

The River Avon winds through the hills more than two miles away from Stonehenge. This river was an important waterway in ancient times and, according to many theories, played an important role in the building and use of Stonehenge.

The wide Avenue, which leads directly to Stonehenge, curves some two-and-one-half miles from the river to the standing stones. Experts debate the purpose of the Avenue. Was it a ceremonial approach to a holy shrine? Was it a pathway to guide the sun up the slope to the monument? Did it serve as a road for bringing sacrificial victims to Stonehenge? Or was it

"Most of what has been written about Stonehenge is nonsense or speculation. No one will ever have a clue what its significance was."

R.J. Atkinson, *Discover* magazine

"The one mistake to avoid is to suppose that one function, or set of functions, must have reigned throughout. We know that Stonehenge was 'active' for at least 1,700 years, and we have only to think of that time-span in our own era to realize the improbability . . . of considerable changes not having taken place."

John Fowles, *The Enigma of Stonehenge*

merely a road used in the construction of Stonehenge, for bringing the giant stones up from the river?

When the Avenue neared the standing stones, it passed what today is called the Heel Stone. Some scientists believe the Heel Stone played a prominent role in the marking of the summer solstice at Stonehenge. Whether this is true or not is one of Stonehenge's many mysteries.

Just past the Heel Stone, the Avenue cut through two earthworks more than three hundred feet in diameter. These two rings of earth surround Stonehenge completely with a break only where the Avenue crosses them. A shallow ditch separates the two rings. Long ago the earthen rings stood much higher and the ditch was much deeper. Erosion has long since smoothed the rings and filled the ditch. Experts have debated the importance of this ditch. Did it represent an early concept of Stonehenge when circles made of piles of earth would hold significance? Or were the rings an integral part of the Stonehenge we know today?

A view of Stonehenge showing Sarsen Stones (outer, capped stones) and bluestones (inner, individual stones).

Just inside the earthen rings, there is a ring of fifty-six holes, possibly dug at the same time as the ditch and embankments. These are now called the Aubrey Holes after the scientist, John Aubrey, who discovered them in the seventeenth century. The holes apparently never held posts or stakes. Their exact use remains a mystery.

Four large stones called Station Stones are set among the Aubrey Holes. What purpose did these four unusual stones have? Were these Station Stones for astronomical observation? One Stonehenge theory suggests so.

Just past the Aubrey Holes is an open area, the "soul" of Stonehenge, the huge standing stones themselves.

The first great ring of stones is the Outer Ring. This is the outermost circle of thirty massive pillars, the main circle of Stonehenge. Each stone in the Outer Ring weighs close to forty tons and stands sixteen feet tall.

A trilithon, two stones capped by a third. The "horseshoe" formed by five of these trilithons is one of the most impressive aspects of Stonehenge.

The Sarsen Stones

Named the Sarsen Stones, these huge stones were once joined together in an unbroken circle at their tops. Without using cement of any kind, the builders of the Outer Ring placed capstone, or lintels, connecting the Sarsens together. Each lintel was individually cut to fit not only atop two adjoining Sarsens, but to interlock with its neighbors like pieces of a puzzle. Six of these giant Sarsens are still united as their builders intended nearly four thousand years ago.

Where did these gigantic Sarsen Stones come from? This is one of the earliest mysteries of Stonehenge. No stones of a similar type are found near Stonehenge or on the surrounding Salisbury Plain. How were they cut and shaped by people who had only wooden mallets for hammers? Most importantly, how were they raised and set in the ground? Opposing theories about these questions will be examined in a later chapter.

Inside the Outer Ring is another ring of smaller stones, each weighing as much as five tons. These rocks are of a different type than the Sarsens. They are called "bluestones" because of their bluish tint.

No such rock is found naturally within 250 miles of Stonehenge. How then were they transported to Stonehenge? Why were rocks from such a great distance even chosen for building Stonehenge? Was the blue color a religious symbol or a sign of power? These are more mysteries with varying explanations.

Inside the ring of bluestones are two horseshoe-shaped groups of stones, one inside the other. Both horseshoes face northeast toward the entrance of the Avenue.

The first horseshoe is made from Sarsen Stones, similar to the Outer Ring in shape but much larger. These giants stand between twenty and twenty-five feet tall and are capped with lintels. Called "trilithons" (three stones), these are the largest of all the stones at Stonehenge. Three of these mammoth trilithons still stand complete.

Just inside this horseshoe is another made of bluestones. At the center of the horseshoe's curve is the Altar Stone, the heart of Stonehenge.

Each of the major parts of Stonehenge—the earth rings, the rings of stones, the horseshoes—were built at different times. Each makes its own contribution to the mysteries of Stonehenge. Each poses its own puzzle. Each reveals different answers to the enigma of Stonehenge.

How Did the Name Stonehenge Originate?

Mysteries even surround the name *Stonehenge*. No one knows what Stonehenge was called in ancient times. It was not until medieval times that Stonehenge received the name it has today.

At various times, the monument has been called

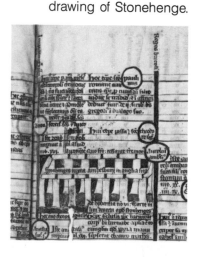

A small segment of the page showing the earliest known drawing of Stonehenge.

Stanheng or *Stanhenge*. *Stan* is the Old English word for "stone." *Henge* comes from the Old English word meaning "to hang." It might have been called this because the lintel stones seem to "hang" in the air from the supporting Sarsens. Thus it was called the place of the "hanging stones," or Stonehenge.

Another possibility is that Stonehenge was named for the hanging of criminals from the lintel stones. Medieval gallows were not the upside down L-shape we think of today. Medieval gallows were two upright posts with a crossbar, the exact arrangement of the pillars and lintels of Stonehenge. Whether or not Stonehenge was actually ever used for the hanging of criminals we may never know, but the shape of the trilithons may have made people think of this kind of "hanging stones."

The Mysteries of Stonehenge

For hundreds of years people have been awed by Stonehenge. From a distance it looks small, standing there alone on Salisbury Plain. But up close the stones seem to rise like giants reaching up to the sky. Nature did not place the stones in this powerful pattern. A remarkable group of people must have wrestled these massive stones into place.

The standing stones speak to us through ages, daring us to seek answers to the questions they pose.

Who were the people who conceived Stonehenge? How did they build this unique ring of stones? Why did they labor for over three hundred years to create Stonehenge?

The huge rocks reveal little, stubbornly giving up clues only to the most determined. Those few clues leave us looking for more, tempting us to find the answers to the riddles they pose. And for each clue uncovered, opposing ideas of its meaning clash in the attempts to solve the mystery of Stonehenge.

"My working hypothesis has gradually developed over the past two years: If I can see any alignment, general relationship or use for the various parts of Stonehenge then these facts were also known to the builders."

Astronomer Gerald S. Hawkins, *Stonehenge Decoded*

"Here are all the elements of a modern myth. We believe in a people like us, creating order the way we do, motivated by the same desires to capture and control nature. . . . But this assumes all humans have lived in a dull, unimaginative, self-centered world in which all people regard nature the same way. . . . We need to look far beyond the measurements and statistics spewed out by the computer, to develop ideas and explanations that have more meaning for the ancients than for us."

Professor Anthony Aveni, *Sky & Telescope* magazine

Two

Who Built Stonehenge?
Lore and Legends,
Fact and Fantasy

We may never know the people who conceived, designed, and constructed Stonehenge because these builders left no written records. The only clues to their thoughts lie in the great stones themselves and in the artifacts recovered from under the ground at Stonehenge. Yet with these few clues, we can piece together a picture of these remarkable people, who, through backbreaking effort and determination, built one of the world's most remarkable structures.

Over the ages many stories and legends about Stonehenge have been fashioned to explain its construction. Some say magic built Stonehenge. Others argue that only the Greeks or Romans had the knowledge and skills to make such a monument. Many now believe that Stonehenge was built by different groups of people over a long period of time.

Sometime in the dim past, the builders abandoned Stonehenge. Maybe another tribe conquered them and absorbed them. Maybe a sudden illness killed many of the local population, forcing the survivors to leave for a healthier climate. The knowledge of the builders

"Giants" is one whimsical answer to the question of who built Stonehenge.

of Stonehenge faded as those who knew the true story passed on.

Before the Middle Ages, few people were concerned with Stonehenge. The daily struggle to survive filled everyone's days, leaving little time for journeys into the countryside in search of wonders. The few travelers who crossed the lonely, windswept Salisbury Plain thought Stonehenge was a natural rock formation. They believed that powerful and mysterious natural forces had pushed and pulled these massive stones into their awesome shape.

Not until the more prosperous and settled times of the Middle Ages did people again become intrigued with Stonehenge. With this interest came wonder. How could such massive stones have been moved? Who would have wanted to move them? Why was Stonehenge built?

An aerial view of Stonehenge.

We ask these same questions today and, although we do not know the complete answers, we seem to be closer to solving the mysteries of Stonehenge than anyone before us.

The scientific investigation of Stonehenge began in the seventeenth century. Until that time only stories and legends explained the existence of Stonehenge. The following two legends from the Middle Ages shed light on how people of that time believed Stonehenge was built. Both tales, while now considered entertaining stories, were once taken to be the truth about the creation of Stonehenge. Interestingly, both legends seem to be rooted in fact.

Merlin's Magic and the Dance of the Giants

Stanhenges, where stones of wonderful size have been erected after the manner of doorways, so that doorway appears to have been raised upon doorway. No one can conceive how such great stones have been raised aloft, or why they were built there.

These few words, written originally in Latin, are the first mention of Stonehenge in written records. They were written in about the year 1130, by the archdeacon Henry of Huntingdon. He wrote a brief history of England in which he described Stonehenge. Henry thought it was an oddity the curious traveler must visit.

Many of the people who journeyed to see Stonehenge believed magicians had erected the great stones. They could not imagine that humans unaided by magical power could have built such a grand and unusual monument. To them only Merlin, the mightiest of the magicians, could have performed such an awesome feat.

The twelfth-century English writer and historian, Geoffrey of Monmouth, first recorded Merlin's building of Stonehenge in his famous book *History of the Kings of Britain.* Geoffrey claimed that his book

"Merlin . . . placed in position all the gear which he considered necessary and dismantled the stones more easily than you could ever believe. Once he had pulled them down, he had them carried to the ships and stored on board, and they all set sail once more for Britain with joy in their hearts. . . . [He] Merlin obeyed the King's orders and put the stones up in a circle round the sepulchre, in exactly the same way as they had been arranged on Mount Killaraus in Ireland, thus proving that his artistry was worth more than any brute strength."

Geoffrey of Monmouth, c. 1136

"It is quite clear that everything [Geoffrey of Monmouth] wrote . . . was made up, partly by himself and partly by others, either from an inordinate love of lying, or for the sake of pleasing the Britons."

William of Newburgh, c. 1190

Above: Merlin, the great magician of legend. Below: This early drawing gives an idea of why the standing stones were called "Dance of the Giants."

was a translation of "a certain very ancient book written in the British language." However, no other scholar or historian of that time or this knows of the existence of such a book.

Geoffrey collected tales and stories, often mixing his own brand of fantasy with fact. Much of what he wrote is based on fact, but where the facts were missing, Geoffrey often supplied details from his imagination.

According to Geoffrey, the great stones of Stonehenge were brought from Ireland to England to mark the burial place of a group of slain British princes. These prince-warriors had been treacherously killed by Hengist, the leader of an army of Saxons who invaded Britain around A.D. 450.

Hengist, determined to defeat the Britons any way he could, had called a truce inviting the British princes to meet with him at his camp on Salisbury Plain. The British, trusting Hengist's promise of peace, came unarmed into the camp. They did not know that each

Hengist, on the left, and his companion Horsa are greeted by a British king.

of Hengist's men had a long knife concealed in the sole of his boot. At a signal from Hengist, the Saxons rose up and cut the throats of four hundred and sixty of the finest warriors in England.

Later, the British King Ambrosius visited the site of the treachery. He wanted to see "where the earls and princes lay buried whom the accursed Hengist had slain." King Ambrosius decided to build a memorial to the slain princes, a memorial that would last forever. However, his own carpenters and stone-masons were unable to build him the monument he desired. So Ambrosius sent for Merlin to work his magic.

Merlin told the king if he wanted to "grace the burial-place of these men with a work that shall endure forever, send for the Dance of the Giants in Ireland. For a structure of stones is there that none of this age could raise save his wit were strong enough to carry out his art. For the stones be big, nor is there stone anywhere of more virtue, and, so they be set up round this plot in a circle, even as they be now set up, here shall they stand forever.''

King Ambrosius laughed at Merlin, wondering how stones of such great size and so far away could be brought to Salisbury Plain.

Merlin answered, ''Laugh not so lightly. In these stones is a mystery. Giants of old did carry them from the farthest ends of Africa and did set them up in Ireland. . . . Not a stone is there that lacketh in virtue of witchcraft.''

Merlin convinced the king. Ambrosius immediately set forth with fifteen thousand men to get the stones. The Irish, unwilling to give up their standing stones without a fight, raised an army to stop the British invaders. The British defeated the Irish army and took control of the Dance of the Giants. Unfortunately, all of the king's men could not budge the giant stones. They could not even pull them down.

Merlin came to their rescue. According to Geoffrey, Merlin ''burst out laughing and put together his own engines [machines] . . . laid the stones down so lightly as none would believe . . . and bade carry them

Geoffrey of Monmouth reported that Merlin magically transported the stones from Ireland to England.

to the ships.'' The ships returned to England and there Ambrosius' men ''set them up about the compass of the burial ground in such a wise as they stood upon Mount Killaraus . . . and proved yet once again how skill surpasseth strength.''

Geoffrey's tale made a good story, explaining to the medieval believer how the stones came to be standing on Salisbury Plain. With his account of Stonehenge, his *History* was one of the most popular books of its time.

Fact or Fiction?

Geoffrey's account has long since been discredited. One contemporary critic, William of Newburgh, wrote, ''It is quite clear that everything this man wrote . . . was made up, partly by himself and partly by others, either from an inordinate love of lying, or for the sake of pleasing the Britons.'' By the late 1800s Geoffrey's *History* was considered by many to be just a ''bare-faced invention, and full of old wives' tales, and idle stories.''

It is interesting to note that, while many of Geoffrey's critics complained of his creating stories, not one medieval scholar criticized the idea that magic

Castlerigg stone circle in Cumbria, England. This is one of many stone circles found in Britain and Europe. Who built them?

was used to transport the stones. Magic was real to the medieval people, scholar and uneducated alike. To them Merlin would have been powerful enough to have created Stonehenge.

Modern historians have noted a curious historical parallel in Geoffrey's account of Stonehenge. His story closely echoes the history of his own time. Shortly after conquering England at the battle of Hastings in 1066, William the Conqueror built a great abbey to commemorate his victory over King Harold.

The abbey's altar was placed above the precise spot King Harold had fallen. Was Geoffrey imitating the history of his own time, transplanting an actual event to explain Stonehenge? Is this why King Ambrosius built Stonehenge on the site where the prince-warriors had perished? To many scholars this appears to be true.

Today we know that Stonehenge could not have been built to honor the slain British princes. By the time Ambrosius became king of Britain in 455, Stonehenge had been standing for over two thousand years.

Yet, 450 ancient burial mounds have been found around Stonehenge. Is it only a coincidence that this number so nearly matches the 460 prince-warriors slain by Hengist? Did Geoffrey know of these mounds and therefore incorporate this number into his history?

Burial Rites

We know that Stonehenge did play a role in burial ceremonies because early in this century archaeologists uncovered ancient human remains at Stonehenge. Thus, long-living legends combined with scientific investigation lead to the conclusion that Stonehenge was, in some still-unknown way, connected to age-old burial rites. In this story and others there seems to be a kernel of truth forming the basis of the tale.

Several other aspects of Geoffrey's tale have a ring of truth. As mentioned earlier, Europe is dotted with hundreds of rings of standing stones. Twenty-five stone rings have been discovered in Ireland alone. Dozens more are scattered about Britain from the isolated Orkney islands of the far north to the southernmost tip of England. It seems quite possible that Geoffrey, knowing of the other stone circles in Ireland, used them in his tale of the origin of Stonehenge.

Some Basis in Fact?

Other details from Geoffrey's book may have also been based on fact. For example, the "fifteen thousand men" who went to Ireland to steal the stones could be the long-remembered people who really did build Stonehenge. The impact of feeding and housing such an army of workers would not be forgotten by the local inhabitants. Stories of this mass of men would have been passed down from generation to generation. And like many other tales based on a real event, the story would have changed slightly with each retelling. Maybe, it is argued, Merlin's thousands were indeed the multitude who actually built Stonehenge. Maybe they did not bring Stonehenge in one piece from Ireland, but in many pieces over many years from a distant location.

What about Merlin's "engines"? Were these engines in fact the rememberance of the simple machines —the logs and sleds, the ropes and pulleys, the boats and barges—used by the actual builders of Stonehenge to transport and raise the heavy stones?

Another interesting aspect of Geoffrey's story is that he described the stones as having come from far away. Was Merlin's Ireland really modern Wales? Wales is to the west of the Salisbury Plain just as Ireland is. The peoples of both countries then and now share many of the same cultural attributes. In people's memories, could the two countries become one? This certainly is a possibility.

A fourteenth-century manuscript shows Merlin popping a lintel into place.

Scientific investigation in the twentieth century has proven beyond a doubt that the famous bluestones of Stonehenge did come from Wales. These stones are identical to those in the Prescelly Mountains in southern Wales, at least 250 miles away from the Salisbury Plain. Somehow these gigantic stones were transported to their present site, a task that must have seemed nearly impossible to the mortals of Geoffrey's time. Why not have magical machines accomplish this formidable job since no one knew the way it was actually done?

Geoffrey's tale has persisted down through the ages because it entertains. While it is not accurate history, there are enough elements of truth in the story not to discount it completely. Mixed into the fantasy are too many facts to ignore. It seems quite possible that Geoffrey captured key folk memories in his tales, memories rooted in actual events.

The Devil and the Heel Stone

Another medieval legend accounts for the building of the ring of Stonehenge and the presence of one unusual stone outside the ring. This legend suggests that the devil built Stonehenge. And like Geoffrey's account, this legend may have some basis in fact.

According to the legend, the stones had been standing on an old woman's property in Ireland. When the devil heard about the great stones, he greedily wanted them for himself.

Disguised as a gentleman in his best clothes, the devil came to make a deal. He piled a great stack of gold coins on the old woman's table, telling her that she could keep all she could count while he moved the stones. The old woman, seeing the amount of gold, immediately agreed to sell the stones. She was certain that the ''gentleman'' could never remove all of the stones before she got all of the gold.

But as she reached for the first gold coin, the devil laughed and said, ''Why should I pay you the gold

now? All of the stones have disappeared.''

The old woman looked at the place where the stones had stood. Indeed they were gone! The devil had spirited them away to England, placing them on Salisbury Plain.

The devil was so pleased with his trick that he bragged, ''No one will ever know how these stones came here, or from where. No one will ever be able to count them all.'' An old priest overheard the devil's bragging and challenged the devil, saying he could count the stones. The devil grew angry at the priest who immediately fled. The devil picked up one of the huge stones and hurled it at the fleeing priest. The priest, running for his life, was hit on the heel by the stone, but was uninjured. Instead his heel dented the stone.

As remarkable as the story sounds, people believed this is how Stonehenge came to stand on Salisbury Plain. It also explained how one huge stone came to stand outside the circle. Intriguingly, this stone has an unusual dent in it, a dent almost exactly the shape

Did the devil trick an old woman and then send the stones to England with his evil power?

of a heel. For centuries the stone has been called the "Heel Stone."

There is another interpretation of how this stone came to stand alone outside the circle. The Heel Stone is the stone over which the sun is spotted during the summer solstice, the longest day of the year. The sun rises over the tip of the Heel Stone only on the dawn of the day of the solstice. Many people believe that the Heel Stone was placed in its present location specifically to make the observation of the sunrise on the morning of the solstice easier.

The Sunstone

In fact, the stone has also been called the Sunstone. The Greek word for sun is *helios*. Thus the name *Heel Stone* is thought to come from *helios stone*. Another interpretation is that it comes from the Welsh word for sun, *haul*, pronounced "hayil." Is this remembrance of the Welsh connection proof that the stone came from Wales?

Numerous other stories, tales, and legends have been told to explain the mysteries of Stonehenge. These two examples demonstrate that although the stories seem fanciful to us today, quite possibly and probably within them lie elements of the truth.

It was not until the seventeenth century that people of science turned their minds to unraveling the

Legend says that the devil threw a huge stone at an impertinent friar, permanently denting the stone.

mysteries of Stonehenge. These architects, doctors, historians, and scientists brought their knowledge and skills to Stonehenge in an attempt to understand who built it and why it was built.

The sun rising over the Heel Stone.

Inigo Jones Surveys Stonehenge

King James I ordered the first real study of Stonehenge. During a visit to the area in 1620, he became intrigued with the monument. The Duke of Buckingham, realizing the King's interest, offered to buy the stones for any price but the owner refused to sell. He did, however grant the Duke permission to dig two deep holes in the center of the stone ring to look for clues to the origin of the monument. The Duke's diggers discovered numerous stag horns, bull

King James I (top) and his friend Inigo Jones (bottom), the architect who first seriously studied Stonehenge.

horns, arrow points, rusty armor, rotten bones (maybe human), and charcoal.

Seeing these artifacts, King James decided that a more intensive study of Stonehenge was needed. He ordered Inigo Jones, his chief architect and Surveyor-General of Works, to draw a plan of the stones. King James also wanted Jones to find out how the stones had come to be here and why. Jones was given "his Majesty's Commands to produce, out of my own Practice in Architecture, and Experience in Antiquities abroad, what possibly I could discover" about Stonehenge.

Inigo Jones was a master architect, having studied architecture throughout Europe. Jones had been especially interested in the Roman ruins in Italy. He therefore looked at Stonehenge through the eyes of an architect with a prejudice toward a Roman influence. He also viewed Stonehenge as a gigantic architectural puzzle which he alone could solve.

Jones visited Stonehenge numerous times, making sketches and diagrams. Before his death in 1652 he reached the conclusion that only the Romans could have built a monument as magnificent as Stonehenge.

The Early Britons

Jones dismissed the early Britons as the builders. Like many others of his day, Jones viewed the ancient Britons as uncouth, ignorant savages. He wrote, "Lacking constant habitations, ignorant of the skills of corn-growing, they squatted in caves, tents, and hovels, living on milk, roots, and fruits. Their priests, the Druids, roused them to worship in groves of trees, having of themselves neither Desire, nor Ability to exercise, nor learn from others . . . Knowledge in the Art of Building."

Had the Romans discovered any grand buildings when they conquered Britain? Jones asked. They had not recorded any such buildings, evidence for Jones to conclude that the brutish Britons could not have built Stonehenge.

Jones then asked who could possibly have built Stonehenge? What ancient craftspeople and architects were capable of building such a massive monument? Who had the skills, mathematics, and knowledge to build magnificient Stonehenge? Who had the machines to move such huge blocks?

Did the Romans Build Stonehenge?

For Jones there was only one answer: The Romans alone possessed such skill and knowledge. He supported his arguments by comparing his drawings of Stonehenge to his drawings of a Roman theater. In both sketches he found a series of equilateral triangles. He found units of measurement which matched. When he added another set of towering stones to the center of his drawings of Stonehenge, Jones saw that the two buildings matched in shape and proportion. Therefore, he claimed the "rarity of invention" and "beautifull Proportions" of Stonehenge could only have been accomplished by the master Roman architects.

When did the Romans build Stonehenge? Jones concluded that the monument was built, "Happily, about the times, when the Romans having settled the Country here . . . reduced the naturall inhabitants of this Island unto the Society of Civill life." This was in the second century.

Jones dismissed Geoffrey of Monmouth's version of the building of Stonehenge. He said King Ambrosius and his people were a "savage and barbarous people, knowing no use at all of garments . . . destitute of knowledge [needed] to erect stately structures, or such remarkable works as Stoneheng." Jones then dismissed Merlin. "As for that ridiculous Fable of Merlin's transporting stones out of Ireland, it is an idle conceit."

Critics immediately pointed out why the Romans could not have built Stonehenge. First, the structure

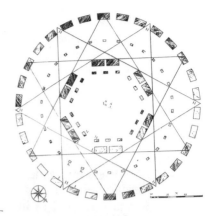

Inigo Jones's drawing of the way he believed Stonehenge looked in its prime. In order to make it fit his theories about the builders, he erroneously added an extra trilithon and changed the arrangements of the stones.

"From many and repeated visits [to Stonehenge], I conceived it to be an astronomical temple."

Dr. John Smith, 1771

"Till some practical astronomer will come forward and tell us in intelligible language what observations could be performed with the aid of the circles of Stonehenge, we may be at least allowed to pause."

James Fergusson, 1872

was too primitive to have been constructed by the sophisticated Romans. Just look at the fine lines and classical proportions of their own buildings. They carried their architecture with them into conquered lands and continued their own building styles wherever they ruled—why not here as well? And where are the traditional Roman inscriptions like those carved onto every other Roman building? Edmund Bolton, a respected historian of the time, wrote, "The dumbness of it (unlesse the letters bee worne quite away) speakes that it was not the workes of the Romans. For they were wont to make stones vocall by inscriptions."

Jones's conclusions about the intelligence of the early Britons have also been shown to be wrong. In the next chapter we will see that these people were indeed quite sophisticated, building huge earthworks, living in organized communities, and having extensive trade with distant lands.

The Druids

Over the centuries almost everyone, scientists and lay people alike, has agreed that Stonehenge was a temple of some sort. The circular shape, the towering stones, and the commanding location indicate to many that Stonehenge was a holy place. But who built it and how they worshipped remains a mystery still.

Over the last three hundred years, the Druids, an ancient religious sect, have been persistently credited with the building of Stonehenge. The Druids were a group of Celtic priests: medicine people, lawgivers, and judges. The Celts were a semi-nomadic, warring tribe that lived in western France. Many Celts migrated to England about the fifth century B.C. The Celts inhabited much of southern England until the Romans, defeating the British tribes of the region, conquered the area two thousand years ago. The Romans, however, never conquered the fierce Celts who fled to the highlands of Scotland and Wales to continue their way of life.

Not much is known historically about the Druids in Britain. The Roman historian Tacitus is the only direct authority we have. Tacitus recorded a Roman attack on the British in A.D. 60. The British were defeated in a fierce battle where their Druid priests ''lifted up their Hands to Heaven, pouring forth most terrible Execrations'' (curses).

In describing the savage British warriors Tacitus wrote, these ''inhuman people were accustomed to shed the Blood of their Prisoners on their Altars, and consult their Gods over the reeking Bowels of Men.'' The Druids were the priests who guided such sacrifices. Clearly, Tacitus was glad the Romans had not lost to such an uncivilized tribe.

Julius Caesar found the Druids of ancient Gaul (France) equally sinister. When he conquered Gaul he found the Druids urging human sacrifice either to appease the gods or to foretell the future.

John Aubrey

It was John Aubrey, a scientist and historian, who first connected the Druids to Stonehenge during his study of the monument in 1663. John Aubrey first visited Stonehenge in 1634 when he was eight years old. He was so fascinated with the massive standing stones that he was determined to learn more about them. Aubrey provided many original ideas about Stonehenge, the most important being his discovery of the ring of fifty-six holes circling the standing stones. But his suggestion that the Druids may have built Stonehenge has remained and been embellished over the last three hundred years.

One of Aubrey's favorite pastimes was the investigation of ancient ruins and monuments. He was a friend of King Charles II, and he took the King to see Stonehenge in 1663. The King was impressed with Stonehenge and the huge Silbury Hill nearby, so impressed that he asked Aubrey to undertake an intensive study of these sites.

John Aubrey, discoverer of the holes that bear his name. Their exact purpose is still debated by scholars and scientists.

Aubrey had already dismissed any notion that the Romans built Stonehenge. He had read Inigo Jones's book and disagreed with his conclusions. He felt that Jones, by adding another tower to Stonehenge and by using variable measurements, had forced the monument to fit his own ideas.

Aubrey spent a great deal of time surveying, sketching, planning, and observing ancient stone structures throughout southern England. He was looking for a pattern in their design and construction.

The Holes

During his fieldwork in 1666 he made an invaluable discovery. He was the first to make note of the fifty-six holes circling the standing stones, the holes which were to be named after him. Aubrey drew no conclusions about the meaning of the holes. It was not until 1921 that their true importance became known during an archaeological dig. It was discovered then that many of the holes contained human bones, signs that Stonehenge had perhaps played some role in ancient funeral rites.

Aubrey proposed that the Druids built Stonehenge. His argument was relatively simple: The Druids were the priests of the ancient Britons, therefore Stonehenge and other monuments were the temples of the Druids. He wrote, ''That the Druids being the most eminent Priests among the Britaines: 'tis odds, but that these ancient Monuments were Temples of the Priests of the most eminent Order, Druids.'' Aubrey went on to say that this was only a possibility. ''Clear evidence [suggests] that these monuments were Pagan-Temples, but it is no more than a 'probability' that they were Temples of the Druids.''

Aubrey's words linked the Druids to Stonehenge in a way no one had done before. Aubrey was well respected the King and his followers, and so his announcement was deemed accurate and important. Although others before had suggested that the Druids were connected with Stonehenge, the impact of Aubrey's conclusions echoes down the centuries to us.

Earlier, Inigo Jones had dismissed the idea that the Druids had built Stonehenge. He argued that the Druids had never been "studious in architecture or skilled in anything else" like architecture. They could not design things, did not know mathematics (which is critical to building a structure the size of Stonehenge), and could not read or paint or sculpt. Jones had reasoned that they had none of the skills necessary for architecture except philosophy and astronomy.

Jones wrote, "In a word let it suffice, Stoneheng was no work of the Druids, or of the ancient Britans; the learning of the Druids consisting more in contemplation than practice, and the ancient Britans accounting it their chiefest glory to be wholly ignorant in whatever Arts."

But the idea that the fearsome Druids worshipped at Stonehenge has taken hold of the imaginations of people seeking an unusual explanation of the origins

Above: A member of the ancient order of Druids. Left: The Druids are shown making a human sacrifice, probably for good luck in battle, while British soldiers look on.

William Stukeley promoted the idea that Druids built Stonehenge.

of Stonehenge. During the next century, one of Aubrey's followers, Dr. William Stukeley, expanded upon the Druid idea, bringing his own fantasies to bear upon the matter.

Stukeley's Fantasies

Dr. Stukeley had long been fascinated with the Druids. He, like Aubrey, had studied Stonehenge. It was Aubrey's idea of the "Templa Druidum," the Druid Temple, which had sent Stukeley to investigate Stonehenge in the first place. Stukeley was so enthralled with the Druids that he called himself Chyndonaxc the Druid among his friends and even created his own druidic ceremonies.

From 1719-24 Stukeley spent weeks studying Stonehenge, walking around the stones, measuring and counting them, sketching them, thinking about them. He dug in nearby burial mounds, accumulating what he considered evidence of the Druids' use of Stonehenge.

In 1740 Stukeley published his book *Stonehenge, a Temple Restored to the British Druids*. Stukeley had carried out careful measurements of the stones and their positions. He is credited with the first mention of "the Avenue," the long road leading down to the River Avon. He made note of the numerous burial mounds in the area around Stonehenge.

Stukeley's Calculations

Stukeley was the first to try to scientifically date the monument instead of using the guesswork done by those before him. Because of the alignment of the stones, Stukeley concluded that the Druid builders must have used a magnetic compass to set out the positions of the stones. Stukeley then used changes in magnetic orientation over the centuries to conclude that Stonehenge was built about 460 B.C.

Stukeley's greatest contribution to the solution of the Stonehenge puzzle was his reference to the astronomical orientation of Stonehenge. His was the first known reference to what has become the most famous single fact about the monument: that the ancient builders had constructed Stonehenge with an eye to the heavens.

Stukeley wrote, "The principal line of the whole work, [points to] the northeast, where abouts the sun rises, when the days are the longest"—in other words, the time of the summer solstice.

Stukeley made some important scientific discoveries about Stonehenge. But his description of his discoveries in his books shows how far he let his imagination run wild. He devised druidical cubits to measure Stonehenge. He called Mr. Hayward, the owner of the property upon which Stonehenge stood, "the Archdruid of this isle." He even made allowances for the druidic custom of human sacrifice as a "most extravagant act of superstition" based upon a misunderstanding of the Bible. Stukeley, in an effort to link the Druids to Christianity, claimed that the Druids were the direct descendants of Abraham.

Stukeley's ideas about the Druids spread. Many other stone rings, standing stones, even natural formations were attributed to the Druids. During the eighteenth century "Druid" temples and other structures were built throughout England, with fantasy supplying what history did not.

Curiosity About Stonehenge

Stukeley's book caused many curious people to visit Stonehenge to see for themselves this temple of the Druids. Why was there no roof over Stonehenge? they asked. "The multitude and nature of their Sacrifices requir'd such Fires as could not admit of Roof or Coverture." Why was Stonehenge round? "The druids were extreamly addicted to Magick, in which Art the circle was esteem'd essentially necessary." Why were the stones of the inner horseshoe not spaced evenly? The answer was that

"Personally I have little use for legends. I much prefer the hard facts."

Gerald S. Hawkins, *Stonehenge Decoded*

"We dismiss primitive superstition rather too easily, forgetting that whatever wrong deductions it may draw, it is in many ways based on a much closer, and finer, perception of natural phenomena than we possess ourselves."

Author John Fowles, *The Enigma of Stonehenge*

this allowed for the different sizes of instruments played by the Druids. What was the large stone lying away from the central circle of Stonehenge? The imaginative replied, that is the Slaughter Stone with its many holes to catch the blood of the victims sacrificed by the Druids. How did the Altar Stone get its name? This was the holy site for the burning of sacrifices. Even the name Merlin was supposed to have druidic origins. It was said to be a version of *Myrddin*, the name of the Celtic god of the sky.

The effects of Stukeley's ideas remain after more than two centuries. In 1781, the Most Ancient Order of Druids was established in London where it still flourishes. (Just look up Druids in the London phone book.) The Druids remain so strongly connected to Stonehenge that this group has been allowed by the

Modern Druids holding a ceremony at Stonehenge.

British government to conduct ceremonies during the summer solstice at Stonehenge.

At midnight the Druids begin their ceremonies with a silent vigil outside the boundaries of Stonehenge. Just as the first light grows strong, about three in the morning, they approach the monument. Solemnly and silently the procession enters Stonehenge. The participants proudly carry the articles of their faith: a cross, a silver cup, sprigs of oak, banners, and a copper ball hanging from three chains. As the sky brightens in the east they march down to the Heel Stone for a prayer. When the prayer ends, they return to the center of Stonehenge and form their own ring. As the sun begins to rise, they raise their voices in a chant. When the full ball of the sun is in view, they raise long bronze horns in the direction of the rising sun and blow them gently. Their worship ends with a ritual at noon, a ceremony marking the sun's zenith on the longest day of the year.

Did the Druids build Stonehenge? Did they ever really worship there? For many believers the answer is yes.

Disagreement About the Druids

Archaeologists argue that it is possible that the Druids did worship at Stonehenge, but they could not possibly have built it. Information from twentieth-century archaeological digging and dating has proven that the stones were standing by 1500 B.C., long before the Druids ever came to Britain. Many scientists also do not believe the modern ceremonies should take place at Stonehenge. They maintain that these ''Druids'' have no real knowledge of what the ancient Druids believed or how they acted. They have no proof that the Druids ever really worshipped at Stonehenge.

Yet every year, as the sun rises over the Heel Stone, the modern Druids are there in their white robes, performing their ceremony honoring the return of the sun.

A Stonehenge Chronology	
3000 B. C.	Nothing on the site
2180	Bank and ditch constructed
2500	STONEHENGE I (Aubrey holes dug slightly later)
1620	STONEHENGE II Construction of Avenue; transport of Welsh bluestone and partial building of double circle; plans changed and sarsen stones erected
2000	Period of stability: most bluestone taken off the site
1500	STONEHENGE III Destruction of dressed bluestone setting and circle-and-horseshoe built
1130 A. D.	First mentioned in manuscript, by Henry of Huntingdon
1136	Geoffrey of Monmouth's history completed
1655	Stone-heng Restored by Inigo Jones
1666	John Aubrey wrote manuscript Monumenta Britannica; Aubrey Holes first mentioned,
1723	William Stukeley discovered The Avenue
1740	Stonehenge: A Temple Restor'd to the British Druids by William Stukeley
1880	Stonehedge: Plans, Description and Theories by Sir William Flinders Petrie published, after most accurate surveys ever conducted (still)
1901	Professor William Gowland's excavations started; erected; admission by payment
1905	First modern Druidic summer solstice ceremony
1918	Stonehenge presented to England by Cecil Chubb
1919-26	William Hawley's excavations
1923	Dr Herbert Thomas announces discovery of source of blue stones, in Prescelly Mountains
1925	Woodhenge's existence revealed by Sq. Ldr. Insall's aerial photography
1953	Professor R. J. C. Atkinson first noticed dagger carvings
1956	Stonehenge by Professor R. J. C. Atkinson published; the classic modern account
1966	Stonehenge Decoded by Professor Gerald S. Hawkins published

A time line showing different periods in Stonehenge's history.

A dolmen grave near Knebel, Denmark. Monolithic structures such as this led Dr. Walter Charleton to believe that Danes might have built Stonehenge.

In 1663 Dr. Walter Charleton wrote a book disputing all other claims about the builders of Stonehenge. Dr. Charleton, physician to the Danish king, decided the Danes had built ''that Gigantick Pile.''

Dr. Charleton based his conclusions upon a similarity between Stonehenge and ancient megalithic tombs in Denmark. These prehistoric graves were long tombs covered with a heavy capstone. Charleton concluded that only the Danes could have constructed such a huge stone circle. ''I conceive it to have been Erected by the Danes, when they had this nation in subjection,'' he wrote. Charleton also argued that Stonehenge was the coronation site for ancient Danish kings. Is not Stonehenge in the shape of the Danish crown? he reasoned.

Charleton did have some historical basis for his theory. The Danes had indeed conquered half of Britain by A.D. 1000. However, the fact that Stonehenge had already been standing for almost two thousand years before the Danes invaded Britain disproves any Danish connection.

Other Possibilities

There are many other minor theories about the building of Stonehenge which bear mentioning, but not in detail. One is that the entire monument, shaped as it is like a crown, was built in honor of King Ambrosius. Ambrosius was discussed earlier in connection with Stonehenge being the burial site of slain British princes.

Another idea is that the massive stones were never quarried anywhere else but instead were ''made'' right there on Salisbury Plain. This theory proposes that the stones were made of crushed rock held together by some marvelous cement.

Others credit the people of the Lost Continent of Atlantis with building Stonehenge.

One theory suggests that the Indians of North

America built Stonehenge (there is a striking similarity between some Indian mounds in America and platform mounds like Silbury Hill near Stonehenge).

Others credit the seafaring Phoenicians or Greeks from the Mediterranean with the building. In fact, there does seem to be some Mediterranean influence in the overall design and construction of Stonehenge. On several of the stones, daggers have been chipped into the rock, daggers that look distinctively Mediterranean in origin. But did the real builders chip these images into the stone or were they carved at a later date? No one knows for sure.

It was not until this century that serious archaeological investigations of Stonehenge were undertaken. Those investigations provided a great deal of new evidence about the real builders of Stonehenge, evidence that disputes many of the previous theories.

An Indian grave mound in the North American Midwest (left) strongly resembles Silbury Hill in England (right). Is there any connection between them?

Three

Who *Really* Built Stonehenge?

Since 1900, three major archaeological expeditions have dug at Stonehenge. Each dig has uncovered new artifacts and information, adding to the knowledge of how Stonehenge was built and who built it. Each investigation has answered old questions and has posed new ones, too. For example, we now know for certain that many of the stones of Stonehenge came from Wales. What we still do not know is why Stonehenge was built. The archaeological clues discovered this century, however, bring us much closer to an understanding of how Stonehenge was built. With this understanding we come close to answering why.

The first major work at Stonehenge this century began not as an effort to discover the secrets of Stonehenge but to preserve the monument. On December 31, 1900, a huge storm swept across Salisbury Plain. The gale-force winds battered Stonehenge, knocking down one of the standing stones. The last time a stone had been toppled by natural forces was in 1797.

Something had to be done to keep Stonehenge standing. Something also had to be done to protect the multitude of visitors who came each year to marvel at the monument. Either the monument had to be

Stonehenge has long had fallen stones, but when an upright stone fell in 1900, measures were taken to preserve the monument.

placed off limits to the public or work had to be undertaken to support any stones in danger of falling.

The first idea was to fence in Stonehenge. Public outcry came immediately. Flinders Petrie, a renowned archaeologist, wrote convincingly to the influential English newspaper *The Times*, ''To do anything to break the marvellous effect of the lonely plain and great masses of stone would be cruel. The sight is the most impressive in England, and on no account should it be destroyed by a hideous iron railing.''

Petrie and others also raised their voices against a suggested restoration of Stonehenge. The supporters of the restoration proposed rebuilding the monument to its original state. Petrie felt that such restoration was the equivalent of lying. He agreed that something had to be done to protect Stonehenge from further human and natural wear and tear, but he objected to fencing and rebuilding.

William Gowland's 1901 excavations unearthed much evidence about the builders of Stonehenge. The men on the right are sifting soil, probably looking for artifacts such as pottery chips and pieces of stone tools.

William Gowland is the man in the middle of this photo. The original builders of Stonehenge may have used ropes and pulleys as part of their construction method.

Most importantly, Petrie wanted to make certain that any excavations would be performed with the utmost care. He insisted that every handful of soil be inspected for artifacts, that all workers be trained in archaeological techniques, that every stone chip or scrap of pottery be marked and recorded, and that the public be kept out of any archaeological digging.

The Society of Antiquaries, who were then responsible for Stonehenge, heeded Petrie's advice. Professor William Gowland, another esteemed archaeologist, became the supervising archaeologist on the project.

Gowland's first excavation was at the base of one of the standing stones which tilted dangerously. The stone had to be supported by a concrete footing. To place the footing, the stone had to be raised and straightened inches at a time. This allowed Gowland a rectangle of only seventeen by thirteen feet in which to dig.

> "The evidence that Stonehenge was designed . . . by a man from Greece is . . . based firstly on Stonehenge itself. . . . Nowhere else in Europe at this time was there a tradition of architectural construction, except in the Mycenean and Cretan civilizations. . . . The inference is, therefore, that a man from one of these civilized countries was responsible for the construction of Stonehenge."
>
> Patrick Crampton, *Stonehenge of the Kings*

> "The new date proposed for the great building period at Stonehenge is 2100 to 1900 B.C.—a time, in other words, when the Mycenaeans themselves were just primitive neolithic farmers. . . . There is no getting around it: the creators of Stonehenge . . . must have been the local inhabitants of Salisbury Plain."
>
> Lionel Casson, *Mysteries of the Past*

Gowland carefully measured each trench before digging. Every bit of dirt was sifted so that no object, however tiny, might be lost. Slowly, painstakingly, Gowland and his men excavated the space beneath the stone.

At first, Gowland found no marvelous treasures. In the top layer he uncovered numerous stone chips, fragments of flint, bottles, and glass, bits of broken pottery, pipe stems, pins, buttons, and other pieces of rubbish from more recent times. He also found ten coins, ranging from a Roman coin more than fifteen hundred years old to a penny from the time of King George III, about 100 years old. This jumbled material was obviously the litter left by centuries of visitors who came to Stonehenge to worship, wander, or wonder.

New Discoveries

As he dug deeper, however, Gowland began to make new, important discoveries. In the chalk rubble at the base of the stone, he uncovered the tools used by some of the builders of Stonehenge! He found the flint axes and hammerstones used to shape and trim the mammoth standing stones. He discovered the deer antler tools used to dig the deep holes in the hard chalk surface into which the standing stones would be placed. He discovered bright green traces of corroded bronze. Gowland wondered if this trace of copper was the remnant of an ornament accidentally dropped. Or was it a coin or medallion placed beneath the stone in homage to a god?

In the cuttings and packings at the base of the stone, Gowland found evidence of how the stone had been erected. He uncovered a deep hole in the chalk layer that had been dug with the antler tools. The hole was straight on one side, but had a sloping ramp on the opposite side so that the massive stone could be slid down the ramp and levered into place in the hole.

No longer were the builders of Stonehenge people

out of legend, but real, struggling, toiling humans who worked with sixty-pound hammers and tough deer antlers to create their monument.

Gowland's month of work revealed more about Stonehenge than all of the guessing of the centuries before. Gowland had discovered how the stones' holes had been dug. He had uncovered the tools used to trim, shape, and put up the Sarsens. He had proved that both the Sarsen and bluestones had been erected at the same date.

Gowland concluded that Stonehenge had been built by Neolithic people who used stone, bone, or wooden tools but who were almost completely without knowledge of metal tools. He wrote, "Had bronze been in general or even moderately extensive use when the stones were set up, it is in the highest degree probable that some implement of that metal would have been lost within the area of the excavations." He concluded that the tiny trace of bronze represented only a rare piece of metal at the site. Gowland believed that Stonehenge was built "during the latter part of

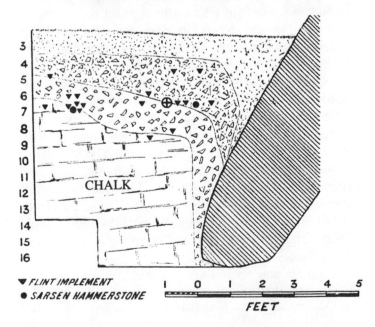

▼ *FLINT IMPLEMENT*
● *SARSEN HAMMERSTONE*

FEET

This drawing shows the general contents of the holes around the giant stones.

At the summer solstice in 1988, modern Druids performed their ceremonies while less reverent "skeptics" looked on. The Heel Stone's "heel" mark can be seen above and to the left of the Druids.

the Neolithic age, or the period of transition from stone to bronze, and before that metal had passed into general use." He estimated that time to be around 1800 B.C.

Temple of the Sun?

Gowland also drew several other conclusions about Stonehenge. He decided that Stonehenge was a temple dedicated to the worship of the sun. How did he reach this conclusion? Gowland believed that the layout of Stonehenge revealed its purpose. The fact that the horseshoe opened to the northeast, toward the summer solstice sunrise, was evidence to him that the people of Stonehenge revered the sun. The alignment of the Altar Stone, Heel Stone, and the Avenue, pointing toward the rising midsummer sun, supported his theory of sun worship.

Gowland dismissed the other exotic theories of Merlin and magic, Greeks, or Romans. He had this to say about the building of Stonehenge: "There is, in fact, no proof [of a foreign origin of Stonehenge], and its plan and execution alike can be ascribed to none other than our rude forefathers, the men of the Neolithic, or it may be, of the early bronze age."

Gowland's evidence and logic swept away other outdated notions of the builders of Stonehenge. It appeared for a time that the fanciful contributions of the Druids, too, were laid to rest. But only momentarily, for in 1905 the Ancient Order of the Druids visited Stonehenge for a secret ceremony initiating seven hundred brothers into the society. Dressed in hooded robes, sporting white "Santa Claus" beards, armed with blindfolds and sickles, the Ancient Order claimed Stonehenge as their heritage chanting,

See, see the flames arise!!
Brothers now your songs prepare!
And ere their vigor droops and dies
Our mysteries let him share!

The Ancient Order was not the only group of Druids to claim Stonehenge for their own during this time. Another band of modern Druids had been celebrating its own rites for years. Problems arose when Sir Edmund Antrobus, the owner of Stonehenge, charged this group an admission fee. They objected, creating an open confrontation when they were caught burying the ashes of their dead brothers on the site. Sir Edmund backed down, but not before the situation brought the problems of maintaining and supervising Stonehenge to the attention of the British government.

In 1913 the government bought the monument to protect Stonehenge and preserve it for future generations. For the first time in its modern history, Stonehenge was no longer owned by an individual but belonged to the British people. However, the disruption of World War I brought excavation and restoration work to a halt.

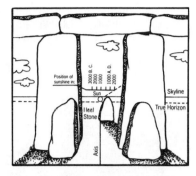

The Heel Stone is shown in alignment with the sun.

Hawley's Finds

The next major archaeological work began in 1919, the year after the war ended. A British government engineer studied Stonehenge, concluding that many of the stones tilted at unsafe angles. In August 1919, the dangerous stones were raised and propped up. Three feet of concrete was then poured to support the stones.

William Gowland had been asked to return to Stonehenge to continue his expert archaeological work, but ill health prevented him from doing so. The job then fell to Colonel William Hawley. Hawley, also a respected archaeologist, had dug at nearby Old Sarum, an Iron-Age stone fort, and had worked to protect many of the other ancient earthworks on Salisbury Plain.

As Hawley worked at the bases of the stones being restored, he uncovered the same kinds of tools and materials that Gowland had found earlier: antler picks,

Old Sarum, another stone circle studied by Col. William Hawley.

stone hammers, flint chips. Hawley also undertook to clear the ditch, in which he found little of interest. He noted finding in one spot "two Sarsen chips, six of foreign stone, seven of bone, three pieces of Romano-British pottery, one flint flake, and a Lee-Enfield cartridge case (from some passing soldier)."

Rediscovering the Holes

Hawley's major find was the rediscovery and excavation of the holes that John Aubrey had discovered back in 1666. Probing with a steel bar, Hawley and his assistant, R.S. Newall, found the fifty-six Aubrey Holes spaced eighteen feet apart and in a complete circle around Stonehenge. Twenty-one of the holes were then excavated.

Newall found the pits to be roughly circular with straight sides and flat bottoms. To Newall the holes seemed to have once held standing stones. The most intriguing discovery was that seventeen holes held cremated bones. A variety of bone pins and flint artifacts were mixed with the bones. Finally, conclusive proof had been uncovered showing clearly that Stonehenge had played a role in ancient burial rites.

Hawley and Newall worked at Stonehenge from 1919 to 1926. Unfortunately, the work was hampered by a tight budget, and excavation was held to a minimum. The archaeologists did make several important contributions to our knowledge of Stonehenge and its builders. The burial use of the Aubrey Holes was made clear, although it remained questionable if the holes had also held standing stones or wooden posts. Hawley and Newall also discovered other holes, called "Y" and "Z" holes. These proved to be of Iron Age origin, dug long after Stonehenge had been completed. They also found additional evidence that the standing stones were Neolithic.

Hawley and Newall knew that they had not answered all of the questions about Stonehenge. Even after digging half the site, they felt they were little closer to an understanding of Stonehenge. Hawley summed up his discoveries, saying "The more we dig, the more the mystery appears to deepen."

During this time, other discoveries about Stonehenge were being made, but not at Stonehenge itself. In 1923, Dr. H.H. Thomas of the Geological Survey solved the mystery of the origins of the bluestones at Stonehenge. In the Prescelly Mountains of southern Wales, Thomas located the three main varieties of bluestone used at Stonehenge. He also showed that the Altar Stone was Welsh, coming from south of the Prescelly Mountains along the return route to Stonehenge. Interestingly, the stones are from near the coast of the Irish Sea, along the shortest sea route to southern Ireland. Remember the Irish connection from both Merlin and the devil's tale.

Aerial Views

Airplanes also helped in the discovery of new material about Stonehenge and the surrounding region. In 1923, aerial photographs of Stonehenge were examined and the Avenue, lost since Stukeley's time, was rediscovered. Two years later another discovery was made from the air. A curious Royal Air Force pilot, G.S.M. Insall, flying over Salisbury Plain,

"I would therefore suggest as probable that when the early inhabitants of this island commenced the erection of Stonehenge, Salisbury Plain was sprinkled over thickly with the great white masses of Sarsen stones and much more sparingly with darker colored boulders (the so-called 'blue stones'), the last relics of the glacial drift, which have been nearly denuded away. From these two kinds of materials the stones suitable for the contemplated temple were selected."

J.W. Judd, quoted in *Megaliths and Masterminds*

"There can thus be no doubt now that it was from this very restricted region [the Prescelly Mountains of Wales] that the bluestones were chosen and brought to Stonehenge."

R.J.C. Atkinson, *Stonehenge*

noticed an earthen ring and ditch with a single entrance. Inside the circle he saw seven closely set rings. Insall, high enough to see Stonehenge at the same time, was intrigued by their similarity.

Woodhenge

Archaeologists immediately began an investigation of this newly found site. They uncovered post holes for huge wooden timbers. They observed that the alignment of the causeway running through the ditch and bank was northeast, toward the rising sun of the summer solstice, identical to that of Stonehenge. At the center of the ring, the excavators unearthed the skeleton of a child with its skull split in half.

This new site seemed so similar to Stonehenge that it was called Woodhenge. Later Insall found another example of a henge, this time in Norwich. Here the post holes were arranged in the open-ended horseshoe pattern, exactly like the setting of the inner Sarsen Stones at Stonehenge. Other henges were discovered, each with its own unique appearance, all sharing some of the same elements. These new discoveries, combined with what had already been found at Stonehenge,

Woodhenge, an ancient wooden circle not found until 1925. Was it a forerunner of Stonehenge?

seemed to support the idea that the henges, including Stonehenge, were sacred sites of long-forgotten rituals.

Digs of the 1950s

The Second World War stopped further excavation and investigation. It was not until the 1950s that another serious archaeological dig was undertaken at Stonehenge. This dig brought to light new discoveries that have further shaped our thinking and knowledge about Stonehenge.

This newest dig began in the spring of 1950. Three experienced archaeologists guided the excavation. Richard Atkinson, the principal archaeologist, had been working on other Neolithic earthworks before coming to Stonehenge. One of his fellow archaeologists, J.F.S. Stone, had just finished digging on the Cursus, a large circular earthwork just north of Stonehenge. Stuart Piggot, an archaeologist from Scotland, had recently discovered Neolithic ritual burial pits similar to the Aubrey Holes. The combined experience and expertise of these archaeologists would help to reveal further the secrets of Stonehenge.

They began digging at the Aubrey Holes. Previously, digs had opened thirty-two of the fifty-six holes. Atkinson and his team excavated two more, but found no traces of post holes. They did, however, confirm that the holes had been dug in the Neolithic era, contained cremated human remains, and—because they held charcoal, bone pins, and flint—could be considered not simple burial spots but pits with a ritual significance.

Atkinson sent a sample of charcoal from one of the holes to Professor Willard Libby in Chicago to obtain a more precise date for the use of the pit. Libby used his newly devised method of radiocarbon dating. This technique measures the decay rate of carbon 14 atoms in a sample such as charcoal. Since carbon 14 decays at a precise rate, a date for the sample can be

Professor Richard Atkinson, one of the most prominent Stonehenge researchers.

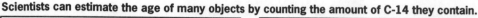

Scientists can estimate the age of many objects by counting the amount of C-14 they contain.

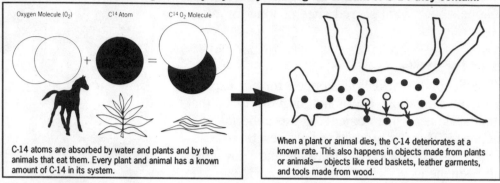

Oxygen Molecule (O₂)   C¹⁴ Atom   C¹⁴ O₂ Molecule

C-14 atoms are absorbed by water and plants and by the animals that eat them. Every plant and animal has a known amount of C-14 in its system.

When a plant or animal dies, the C-14 deteriorates at a known rate. This also happens in objects made from plants or animals— objects like reed baskets, leather garments, and tools made from wood.

The carbon 14 method allows scientists to date ancient materials with relative accuracy.

obtained by checking the amount of carbon 14 still present in the sample. Professor Libby dated the charcoal, at 1,848 years B.C., plus or minus 275 years, giving the archaeologists their first clear scientific dating for Stonehenge. This date closely fit the dates of 200 to 1500 B.C. that archaeologists had already established for Neolithic cultures in England.

As tempting as it was, Atkinson and his team refrained from extensive digging at Stonehenge. Half of the site had already been excavated by Newall and Hawley. Atkinson felt that they should disturb as little more as possible, leaving the site for future generations of archaeologists who would have more refined excavating tools and techniques. They turned instead to reexcavating some of Hawley's trenches and reexamining Hawley's finds and his records.

Bronze-Age Daggers

Then Atkinson made a major discovery without even turning a shovelful of dirt. One of his jobs during the 1953 digging season was to photograph all of the stones. One July afternoon he was waiting to photograph a bit of seventeenth-century graffiti on one stone. Atkinson wanted the late afternoon sun to highlight the carved letters IOH: LVD: DEFERRE so that he could photograph them better.

As he focused his camera on the letters, he noticed some other marks below the graffiti. Upon examination he discovered the shape of a short dagger chipped into the stone. Nearby, he spotted the carvings of four axes. To his astonishment the axes were the flat type typical of the Bronze Age. Two days later ten-year-old David Booth, son of one of the excavators, found another axe. Over the summer a dozen other axes were discovered.

The axes were definitely prehistoric with a broad cutting edge known to be used in Ireland and Britain from 1600-1400 B.C. The archaeologists had found one new bit of evidence dating the creation of Stonehenge. Most important, however, was the dagger which Atkinson had originally spotted. The dagger had a straight, tapering blade, a short hilt, and a wide pommel. This type of dagger was unknown in northern Neolithic Europe. Yet it had an uncanny similarity to daggers unearthed in the royal graves of Greece.

For many scientists this became conclusive proof of Greek influence at Stonehenge. They likened it to a maker's mark or signature of the architect who created Stonehenge. Others disagreed, questioning how such a conclusion could be reached from an eroded dagger shape. Might it not have been carved onto the stone long after the monument had been erected? they asked.

Debate over Dates

Either way, the dagger did help pinpoint another date for the building of the Sarsen stones at Stonehenge. This type of dagger had to have been carved by someone familiar with it in his homeland. For Atkinson and his team, this set the date after 1470 B.C., about when these weapons first made their appearance in Greece.

This theory, however, was disproven in the 1960s by more precise radiocarbon dating techniques which

Carvings of daggers and axes have been found on some of these standing stones. The carvings show a definite knowledge of Mediterranean Bronze Age tools.

"Among the most exotic of the objects found in Wessex graves, chiefly those of women, are small ribbed beads of blue faience. . . . Careful examination leaves little doubt that these beads are of Egyptian manufacture, and their sporadic occurrence both in Crete and on the Atlantic coasts of Iberia and France suggests forcibly that the reached Britain by sea."

R.J.C. Atkinson, *Stonehenge*

"The faience beads of the Wessex culture are no longer of much value for dating. In the first place, statistical analysis of a chemical examination of their composition suggests that they may be significantly different from the majority of beads in the east Mediterranean. . . . Even if the faience beads were imports, they would be of little use for dating, since the manufacture of such beads occurred over such a long period of time in the east Mediterranean."

Colin Renfrew, *Before Civilization*

showed that the first building at Stonehenge had actually been around 2600 B.C. instead of around 1800 B.C.

The new dates, while changing the timeframe of the building of Stonehenge, did not change the sequence in which Stonehenge was built. Atkinson, working carefully on small patches, had finally established the sequence of the three major portions of Stonehenge. In his outstanding book *Stonehenge*, he set forth his ideas of how and when Stonehenge was built. He called the three different building phases Stonehenge I, II, and III, explaining just what happened during each phase and how each phase fit into the overall structure of Stonehenge.

The First Builders

Southern England had long been occupied before the first stone was laid at Stonehenge. Archaeological evidence such as bone harpoons and fishhooks, flint arrowheads, and stone axes shows southern England had been occupied for thousands of years before the construction began at Stonehenge. These early peoples probably lived in shelters made from branches, wore animal skin clothes, and used deer antlers for weapons and tools. These first Britons lived a precarious existence, unable to store up food against future need, living from day to day much as Australian aborigines lived early in this century.

Then a new group of people crossed the North Sea and landed in Britain. These newcomers brought a revolutionary way of life to Britain, for they were farmers and herders. First settling near the coast, these people gradually moved farther inland, eventually reaching the Salisbury Plain. They still hunted and fished for food but lived mainly by their crops and herds. Today we call these people the Windmill Hill culture, named for one of their encampments at Windmill Hill some eighteen miles north of Stonehenge.

These nomadic herders had originally built cir-

cular enclosures of wood to protect their flocks from danger. But over the years the people began to construct more permanent structures: large circular banks and ditches built up from and dug out of the earth. These were for greater protection from wild animals as well as human enemies. To keep danger at bay, these enclosed earthen encampments had only one entrance which could be easily guarded. Several of these circular "camps" were near Stonehenge. The large earthen circular embankment of Stonehenge is just like these early encampments.

The tools of the Windmill Hill people were still primitive flint scrapers and arrowheads, bone needles, crude pottery, and stone axes. They used no metal and are thus considered Neolithic. They did, however, build the long burial barrows scattered over southern England, ten of which are within two miles of Stonehenge. Most of these barrows are over one hundred feet long. Several extend over three hundred feet. By the amount of work it took to construct the barrows, it is clear to archaeologists that the Windmill Hill people were highly organized and could work on building projects over a long period of time.

Early Britons evolved from Neolithic hunters to Windmill Hill herders to Wessex traders. Scientists debate what part each group may have played in Stonehenge's evolution.

Archaeologists have found no clear proof that the Windmill Hill people ever took part in the construction of Stonehenge. However, they do believe the concentration of long barrows and other earthworks built by the Windmill Hill people in and around Salisbury Plain indicates that they treated this region with interest and respect.

The first Britons were gradually absorbed by the Windmill Hill people. British archaeologists call this group Secondary Neolithic, for, like their ancestors, these tribespeople hunted, fished, farmed, and herded without metal tools and weapons.

These people also added something new to the landscape, the henges. Neither cattle enclosures nor fortresses, these circular henges vary in size. The smallest one, only twenty-six feet across, is near Stonehenge. The largest, not far way, near Woodhenge, has a diameter of fourteen hundred feet. Although archaeologists can not be certain, they assume that the henges were associated with religious ceremonies. It was a group of these secondary Neolithic people who built the first henge at Stonehenge.

Stonehenge I (c. 3100 B.C. to c. 2300 B.C.)

Stonehenge I was a large open-air circle almost one hundred yards across. A dirt bank six feet high and a ditch seven feet deep and ten to twenty feet wide made the circle. The ditch had been dug with deer antler picks and shovels made from the shoulder blades of oxen. A number of these primitive but effective tools have been unearthed at Stonehenge. Hawley found eighty picks in one section of the ditch. Other tools made of bone or wood were probably used as well but have since rotted away. Radiocarbon testing of these picks show a date of about 3100 B.C. for this early phase of construction.

Copies of the ancient tools have been made and found to be surprisingly efficient for digging through

Early Britons wore elaborate blue tattoos. If they considered the color blue sacred, perhaps that would explain why they went to such trouble to make bluestones part of Stonehenge?

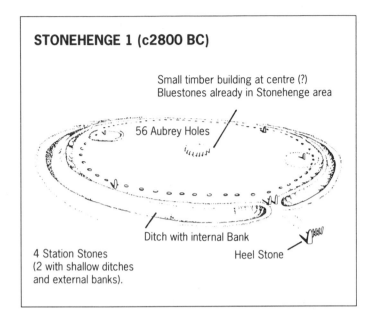

STONEHENGE 1 (c2800 BC)

Small timber building at centre (?)
Bluestones already in Stonehenge area

56 Aubrey Holes

Ditch with internal Bank

Heel Stone

4 Station Stones
(2 with shallow ditches
and external banks).

The first stage of Stonehenge was quite simple: It had two circular embankments separated by a ditch. The Aubrey Holes were dug and the Heel Stone was in place. There may have been a wooden structure in the middle.

the topsoil and chalk of the Salisbury Plain. A modern worker using a modern pick and shovel could excavate a cubic yard of chalk in a seven-hour day. Surprisingly, that same worker took only nine hours to dig a cubic yard using a primitive deer/antler pick and ox-shoulder shovel!

The fifty-six Aubrey Holes were dug during this time. The holes, about eighteen feet apart, make a circle just inside the bank. The original purpose of the holes remains a mystery, for they apparently never held either wooden or stone posts. They appear to have been filled in soon after they were dug, around 3100 B.C. Hawley and Atkinson both found cremated human remains in the holes they excavated. Dating of these remains places some of the burials at 2300 B.C., long after the holes had originally been dug.

Other cremations have been uncovered in the ditch and the embankment. Are these cremations evidence that Stonehenge was an ancient ceremonial cemetery? Or was the embankment simply an easy place to

The famous Heel Stone.

dispose of the dead? Even today this remains one of Stonehenge's untold secrets.

A broad entrance way is cut through the embankment. This entrance faces northeast, almost towards the rising sun at the summer solstice. Two large stones stood on either side of this entrance. Archaeological investigation also revealed the four post holes for a tall wooden archway sixty-five feet away from this entrance.

The Heel Stone, the only stone still standing from Stonehenge I, faces the entrance. This huge stone, weighing thirty-five tons, had been transported twenty miles from the Marlborough Downs before being erected at Stonehenge. This was the first of the great stone movings in the building of Stonehenge.

The Heel Stone once had a companion stone beside it. This second stone was discovered during an emergency excavation in 1979 when the tourist parking lot was extended. Were these two stones another archway? Did they mimic or copy the wooden archway? Did they serve another purpose? Were the stones a way of preserving the archway permanently because stone would not rot like wood? Although there are many theories as to the purpose of these stones, no one is exactly sure of their original use.

Stonehenge II (c. 2150 to c. 2000 B.C.)

From his archaeological investigation Atkinson concluded that sometime around 2150 B.C. the entrance to the circle at Stonehenge had been changed. Part of the ditch was filled to realign the opening which was widened and shifted slightly to the east. The entrance had previously faced northeast, but it did not exactly match up with the sunrise of the summer solstice. Atkinson assumed the builders of Stonehenge II shifted the entrance more to the east to better match the solstice sunrise.

This alignment of the entrance with the summer solstice sunrise would be extremely important if

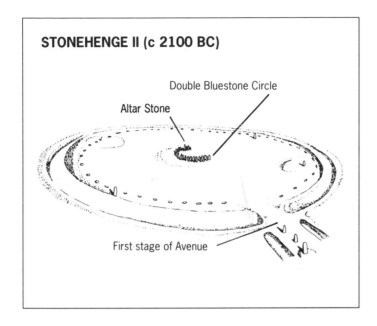

STONEHENGE II (c 2100 BC)

Double Bluestone Circle

Altar Stone

First stage of Avenue

During Stonehenge's second stage the builders erected two concentric partial circles of bluestones and several single standing stones that may have been used for astronomical alignments.

Stonehenge had been a place to worship the sun.

The forty-foot-wide Avenue was built at this time. Aligned with the new axis of the entrance, the two parallel banks and ditches of the Avenue stretched some five hundred feet. Although the Avenue did not run the two miles to the River Avon as it does now, it, too, faced the rising of the midsummer sun.

It was during this phase of building that the first rings of stones, the bluestones, were erected. Atkinson speculated that the blue color of the rocks had a particular significance for the builders. These early people favor bluestone in making ceremonial hand axes. Bluestone was also used in burial rites. Chips of bluestone have been found in numerous graves throughout southern Britain.

It is not known if bluestone had a religious significance. One theory, advanced by author John Fowles in his book *The Enigma of Stonehenge*, is that these early people worshipped the sky and placed a high value on any bluish-colored rock. We know the Celts tattooed their arms and legs with designs etched in blue and painted themselves with blue dyes. Whether earlier peoples began this tradition and the Celts simply copied it remains a mystery.

Bluestones

The bluestones were large flat slabs, shaped naturally by the wind and weather. A tremendous amount of labor went into obtaining the bluestones for no such stone is found near Stonehenge. For centuries people speculated about the origins of the bluestones.

The particular bluestones used at Stonehenge are found within a one-square-mile area on Mount Prescelly in Wales. The natural stones are irregularly shaped, tall columns or flat slabs, sometimes rising forty feet above the ground. Mount Prescelly, wind-blown and dome shaped, is a landmark for sailors on the Irish Sea. The unmistakable weathered shapes of the bluestones can be seen for miles out to sea, helping ancient sailors pinpoint their location on the open water. The wind and weather toppled many of these columns, scattering the broken pieces over the slope.

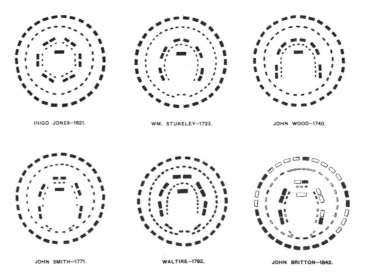

INIGO JONES—1621. WM. STUKELEY—1723. JOHN WOOD—1740.

JOHN SMITH—1771. WALTIRE—1792. JOHN BRITTON—1842.

Six early authorities' ideas of what Stonehenge must have looked like in its prime.

Many of these fallen giants eventually became the bluestones standing at Stonehenge.

From the burial cairns and hilltop forts nearby, it is clear to archaeologists like Professor Atkinson that Mount Prescelly held a particular significance for Neolithic and Bronze Age people. Before, during, and after the building of Stonehenge, these rugged, isolated mountains were used for burials and for protection from enemies. Atkinson and others thought that Mount Prescelly may have played a role similar to that of Mount Olympus in the traditions of the Greeks.

The name *bluestone* is most fitting for this unusual rock. When cracked open, a bluestone glimmers with crystals scattered throughout a blue background. Even today these distinctive bluestones can be found only in the Prescelly Mountains, just as they were four thousand years ago. Professor Atkinson said about the discovery of their source, "There can thus be no doubt now that it was from this very restricted region that the bluestones were chosen and brought to Stonehenge."

Mysterious End to the Construction

The builders of Stonehenge had to bring these huge, heavy stones over 250 miles to the Stonehenge site. Each of the bluestones weighed nearly five tons. Unlike the devil in the early tale, they could not make them fly. No other prehistoric people had accomplished the moving of such heavy stones. Instead, they had used smaller rock from quarries near their building sites. The only other similar effort was to be the moving of the Sarsen Stones to Stonehenge during a later phase of construction.

After all the backbreaking work of moving the bluestones to Stonehenge, the builders suddenly stopped the construction around 2000 B.C. A double circle of holes had been dug and many of the stones placed. However, for some mysterious reason, the circles were not completed. The massive stones that

"Carved on the inner surface of Sarsen Stone number 53 is what seems to be the life-size representation of the square-hilted, diamond-bladed dagger emblematic of Mycenaean royalty, the same buried in the shaft graves of Mycenae about 1500 B.C."

Leon E. Stover and Bruce Kraig, *Stonehenge*

"[The dagger,] if it really is Mycenaean in form, has no more chronological significance than the signature of Byron on one of the marble columns of the Temple of Poseidon at Sounion."

Colin Renfrew, quoted in *Stonehenge Complete*

The building of Stonehenge has been compared to the building of the Pyramids.

had already been erected were removed and all of the holes filled in.

One theory suggests that these people were driven from Salisbury Plain by another tribe who later abandoned the site. Another idea is that many of the workers died from disease and there simply were not enough people left to finish the construction. In either case, why were the bluestones removed and their holes filled? We have no clues. This remains another of Stonehenge's many mysteries.

Stonehenge III (c. 2000 B.C. to c. 1100 B.C.)

The towering stones of Stonehenge with which we are most familiar were erected during the final stage of construction. These are the gigantic Sarsen Stones capped with the horizontal lintels.

The quarrying, transporting, and erecting of the great stones took an immense amount of time and labor. Such a coordinated project needed more than just the hundreds of workers actually building Stonehenge. An undertaking this size needed a community with enough wealth to raise or buy the food and housing necessary for so many workers over such a long period of time.

It was not until around 2100 B.C. that a great deal of wealth existed in southern Britain. Prior to this time the economy had been mainly based on agriculture and herding. People barely existed from one farming season to another. There was little time to perfect arts and crafts or to accumulate large quantities of goods, although some minor trade with distant peoples occurred.

Around 2100 B.C., however, this changed. A group of farmers and traders whom the archaeologists call the Wessex culture became dominant in the region. Why did such a group prosper on the Salisbury Plain? One of the main reasons is the geography of the region. The hills of the downs meet on Salisbury Plain. Prehistoric people naturally traveled along these hills, avoiding the numerous streams running in the valleys below. These ancient roads, known as ridgeways, crisscrossed southern England, many of them converging on Salisbury Plain.

The Wessex people living in the Stonehenge area became well-organized traders because they lived where the ridgeways met. They were able to control the trade routes throughout southern Britain. Their trading network also reached beyond Britain to faraway lands. Beads from Egypt, gold and bronze from Ireland, and amber from Scandinavia have been found in burial mounds on Salisbury Plain.

These traders grew more prosperous than any of their ancestors. And so did the tribes with whom they traded. No longer was everyone just living from day to day. There was enough wealth for people to indulge in luxuries. There must also have been enough food for the population to grow, and enough food so that large numbers of people could be put to work, not in producing more food, but in building huge burial mounds and monuments such as Stonehenge and Woodhenge.

Wealth and Power Ensures Labor

It appears that the wealth and power became concentrated in the hands of a few people. Such wealth and power could command the labor necessary to haul and raise the massive stones of Stonehenge.

During this building phase the tall Sarsen Stones, trimmed and pointed at the bottom, were set up. Five huge lintel stones, placed upon the five trilithons, joined the stones in a horsehoe formation. Thirty smaller upright stones, capped with lintels, formed the outer circle.

The time period for this construction was relatively brief. Within about one hundred years the major portion of Stonehenge proper, the gigantic standing stones and lintels, had been completed. Thus about four thousand years ago the central part of Stonehenge

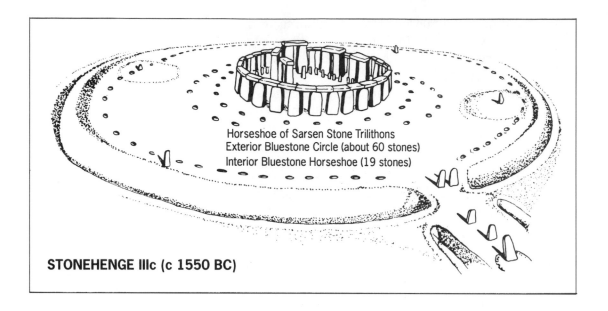

Horseshoe of Sarsen Stone Trilithons
Exterior Bluestone Circle (about 60 stones)
Interior Bluestone Horseshoe (19 stones)

STONEHENGE IIIc (c 1550 BC)

During Stonehenge's third major phase its builders gave it the appearance we see today. They erected the complete circle of thirty large standing stones capped by a continuous lintel of massive horizontal stones. In the center, they built the impressive horseshoe of trilithons.

stood magnificently on Salisbury Plain.

From about 2000 B.C., until about 1100 B.C., only minor changes were undertaken at Stonehenge. Some new stones were added, most notably twenty bluestones set up within the Sarsen horseshoe. Some of these bluestones were then taken down and moved again. Around 1000 B.C. the Avenue was extended all the way to the River Avon.

But Who Built Stonehenge?

Even with the best archaeological tools at our disposal we may never know just who built Stonehenge. Different groups added or removed stones during the three major building phases. While obviously master architects, the people of Stonehenge left no written records. What we do know we have pieced together from the evidence and artifacts they left behind, the bone and stone tools uncovered at Stonehenge as well as the axes, daggers, jewelry, and pottery found in burial mounds scattered over Salisbury Plain.

Much of the mystery therefore remains. Was it one creative genius who conceived Stonehenge? If so, how were the plans transmitted down the ages? Or did many minds contribute to its development? Only further archaeological exploration of Stonehenge and other megalithic sites will provide us with additional clues.

But another mystery remains. How did these early people quarry, transport, and raise these gigantic stones? An examination into their transportation and building methods reveals a great deal more about the building of Stonehenge.

Four

How Was Stonehenge Built?

After years of research archaeologists have pieced together many of the methods used to build Stonehenge in its three stages. In each stage primitive tools and techniques were used with remarkable success.

The first stage of building at Stonehenge, the digging of the ditches and the building of the banks, was relatively simple but backbreaking. Archaeologists have unearthed an abundance of deer antler picks, ox-shoulder shovels, and flint hammers from this stage. Other tools used, such as leather or reed baskets and ropes, have long since rotted away.

Laying out the circle shape of Stonehenge would have been easily accomplished by the builders of circular henges. Archaeologists suggest that once the diameter of the embankment had been decided, the architects of Stonehenge I tied a cord half that length to a pole stuck in the ground. A sharp stick or antler was tied to the other end of the cord. The cord was pulled to its full length and the sharp point scratched through the soil. Using this method it would not take long to etch an accurate circle in the dirt. This circle marked the boundary of the ditch. Although no evidence of this etching remains, archaeologists feel confident that this simple technique was most likely used to create the great circle of Stonehenge.

Who were the real builders of Stonehenge? They were not one group of people, because the building took place over two thousand years.

Even primitive people knew how to create circular structures. This picture illustrates one way the original designers of Stonehenge may have done it. Much like using a school compass, the circle maker would put a stationary post in the middle of the desired area and then use a sharp stick, attached to a rope or cord, to inscribe the circle.

Now came the hard work. The sharpened antler picks were hammered into the hard chalk of the ground at the site. By turning and twisting the antlers, chunks of chalk were pried loose. The broken chalk, shoveled into baskets with the ox-shoulder shovel, was carried to the bank and dumped.

Archaeologists figure that for each digger two chalk carriers were needed to haul away the chalk. They have calculated that the diggers removed over thirty-five hundred cubic yards of earth and chalk to dig the ditch and build the banks. This means that one hundred diggers and two hundred carriers could have completed the ditch in only thirty-five days.

It is quite possible then that the ditch and banks of Stonehenge I were completed in one summer.

But the ditch and bank are not the most impressive features of Stonehenge; the standing stones are. How then did the stones get to Salisbury Plain and how were they erected?

The Builders

Over the years many theories have been suggested as to how the massive bluestones were moved to Stonehenge and then raised. Credit is claimed for Merlin's mighty ''engines'' and the devil. Other explanations included giants from Africa, the Druids and the Roman or Greek builders. But as we've seen, each of these ideas is more fantasy than fact.

If the archaeological evidence collected in this century is correct, farmers and traders built Stonehenge. But just how did they do it?

Once again it has been the archaeologists like Richard Atkinson who have developed the most plausible theories about how the giant stones were moved hundreds of miles and then lifted to stand for centuries.

The archaeological evidence suggests that the traders and farmers of southern Britain were not as primitive and backward as people once believed. From their extensive trade routes, their intricately worked gold ornaments, and their massive monuments, these people are now viewed as being highly organized, skilled in many crafts, and able to work with sophisticated mathematical concepts.

Moving the Bluestones

Once it was established that the bluestones came from Wales, the next question became how were they transported?

There have been theories about how these and other heavy stones were transported to Stonehenge. The most plausible method, proposed by Professor Atkinson, seems to have been a system of rollers on land and rafts on water.

''Stonehenge is now acknowledged as the classic battleground of archaeology, where scholarly reputations are sacrificed and where every new generation massacres the theories of its predecessors.''

John Michell, *Megalithomania*

''Science, however interesting its discoveries, however painstaking its practitioners, cannot explain the total experience of Stonehenge; . . . the effect it still has—even in today's adverse conditions—on most visitors.''

John Fowles, *The Enigma of Stonehenge*

Tools such as these were found in excavations at Stonehenge. The antler pick would have been used to laboriously chop out the hard chalk earth at the site. The shoulder blade shovel would have been used to move debris out of the holes.

After the right stones had been selected, they were apparently placed on sleds with wooden runners. The sleds were then rolled over logs. A long line of logs was put on the ground. As the stones passed, the last log was picked up and carried to the front where the stones rolled over it again. This was repeated over and over until the stones were rolled the sixteen miles to the sea.

The early builders of Stonehenge did not use the wheel because they did not know about it. No evidence of the use of the wheel during the time of the building of Stonehenge has been discovered. Even though the ancient Egyptians knew about the wheel, they did not use it in transporting the heavy stones for building their pyramids. They, too, used the method of rolling the stones over logs.

Moving the Stones

In 1954 a team of archaeologists set out to duplicate the methods they thought the builders of Stonehenge used. These experimenting scientists made a 3.5 ton replica of a bluestone out of concrete. They lashed it to a wooden sled. It took thirty-two strong men to pull the bluestone up a slight slope. Log rollers were then placed under the sled. It took only twenty-four men to move the heavy stone this way. After much

Most authorities think that Stonehenge's builders used some kind of roller system for moving many of the huge stones from their original sites to Stonehenge.

It is possible that the massive bluestones were transported from the Prescelly Mountains by raft.

experimentation, the archaeologists learned that sixteen people were needed for each ton of rock moved. But these could only move the huge stones less than a mile a day!

Experimenting with Methods

The scientists then tried to move their stone by water. They made three small canoes out of wood and joined them together with large boards. They loaded their bluestone onto the raft. The raft lowered only nine inches and needed only four men to pole it along in shallow water. One experiment showed that a single boy could move the raft in quiet water. Although the experimenters did not try to move the raft in deep water, they assumed that the builders of Stonehenge used oars and sails on deep open water away from shore. Thus, the archaeologists concluded, the bluestones were moved the two hundred and fifty miles to Stonehenge, by land and water, by rolling and rafting.

The Sarsen Stones, which were erected during Stonehenge II, were not brought from Wales. These huge stones needed only to be transported about twenty miles. One possible way to have moved the stones was by pulling them on huge sleds. This would most likely have been accomplished in winter when snow covered the ground, allowing the sleds to slide more easily. Another possible method might have been to move the Sarsens south to the River Avon and then raft them to within two miles of Stonehenge. The rest of the journey would have been by rollers.

One scientist, Patrick Hill of Carleton University in Canada, theorized that the builders dammed the River Avon to make the water deeper and thus make it easier to move the heavy stones. Today the river is only two feet deep, not enough for floating and moving such heavy loads.

The Sarsen Stones weigh about thirty tons each. They are about six times larger and heavier than the bluestones. An experiment in moving these stones showed that it took sixteen people per ton to move them. This means that around five hundred people were needed to pull each stone. Probably another two hundred workers cleared the road of rocks and brush

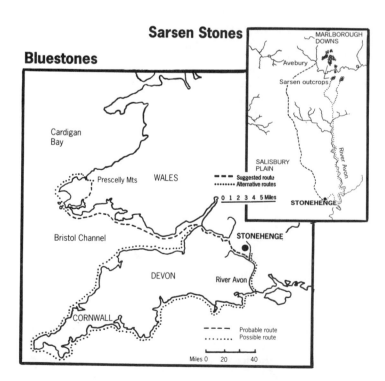

This map shows probable routes for moving the bluestones and Sarsen Stones to Stonehenge.

and laid out the log rollers. It would have taken seven years of intensive labor for these workers to move the rocks to Stonehenge.

Winter Dark

Patrick Hill theorizes that the heavy stones were moved only in the winter when the ground was frozen and ice-covered. The quarry of the Sarsen Stones is uphill from Stonehenge. For seventeen of the twenty miles the slope is long and gentle. Hill says that on smooth ice and down the gentle slope of the land, twenty-five people could have moved the heavy stones.

He also reasons that chores were fewer in winter, and people had more time on their hands to devote to moving the stones. The stones might have been moved a certain distance one year and then left in the spring. The next winter they would be moved farther and then left. Each year this pattern was repeated until the stones reached Stonehenge.

Gerald Hawkins, author of *Stonehenge Decoded*, wrote this about the moving of the stones: ''Whichever routes were taken, for bluestones as well as for Sarsens, and whatever methods of transport were used,

Patrick Hill believes the heavy stones may have been moved in winter when the natural slipperiness of snow and ice could have been used to slide them along.

the moving of the great stones from the Marlborough Downs and Wales to Stonehenge must have been a major undertaking for a good part of the population of southern England.''

Shaping the Stones

In addition to the massive effort to move the stones, an even greater effort was used to shape them. Once the stones reached Stonehenge they had to be cut into the right size and shape for the monument. Some of the shaping was probably done at the quarry sites for there was no need to transport any more stone than necessary for the building.

One method that may have been used in shaping the stones was driving wooden wedges into cracks in the stones. Water would be poured over the wedges, causing them to swell and split the stone. Such stonesplitting has been used by stoneworkers for thousands of years and could well have been used at Stonehenge.

A variety of techniques may have been used to shape and finish the stones. Top left: wedge and water; top right: pounding cracks with stone mauls; bottom left: chiseling the surface; bottom right: smoothing the surface by rolling it back and forth over a Sarsen Stone covered with flint chips.

Another method might have been to chip a long groove in the stone. The stone would then be heated over a large fire. Cold water would be poured on the hot rock. The stone would then be hit by heavy rocks called mauls until it cracked along the line. Some of the ancient mauls, weighing sixty pounds, have been excavated at Stonehenge. In the 1700s William Stukeley reported seeing local stonesmiths crack rocks using just such a method. This method could well have been used three thousand years earlier in shaping the stones of Stonehenge.

Modern experiments have shown that a strong man can chip off six cubic inches of stone in an hour. Professor Atkinson, the archaeologist, figures that three million cubic inches of stone were removed from the Sarsens alone. That means that five hundred thousand hours of hard labor went into just roughly shaping the stones.

Those that were shaped and polished needed additional thousands of hours of labor to chip, grind, and smooth them. To get the right shape, the stoneworkers chipped long shallow grooves into the stones about three inches deep and nine inches wide. These grooves usually ran the length of the stone. The ridge left between the grooves was then hammered out. If the stone was the desired shape already, no further work was done.

Some stones were given a high degree of polish. Heavy Sarsen Stones were pulled back and forth across them, grinding down any rough spots. Hawkins suggests that crushed flint was probably mixed with water and used as an abrasive. Not all the stone had a final shaping and polishing. Many were left in their rough state.

Erecting the Stones

After the stones were cut and shaped, they had to be stood on end and firmly fixed into the earth. Hawley and Atkinson, digging at the base of several

"The method of transport [of the Sarsen stones] to Stonehenge must certainly have been by sledge-hauling overland all the way, for there is no possible water route. . . . There is no certain evidence, of course, for the route actually followed, but [the one I suggest] is certainly possible, and even probable, since it is the only route which avoids excessively steep falling and rising slopes without deviating far from a direct line."

R.J.C. Atkinson, *Stonehenge*

"Atkinson's suggested route keeps to the dry downland. . . . Others have believed the Avon valley, although wetter and wooded, would have been an easier route, using rafts or wooden trackways."

Christopher Chippindale,
Stonehenge Complete

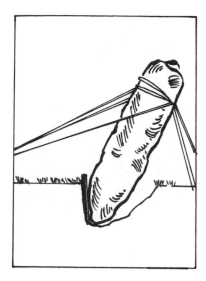

Evidence shows that the giant stones were tipped into their slanted holes by means of ropes or levers.

of the stones, discovered evidence that showed that with much digging and pulling, the gigantic stones could have been raised by simple methods.

The builders of Stonehenge shaped the bottoms of the stones to a dull point. This was for two reasons. first, the pointed end would stick more firmly into the ground. The second reason was that final adjustments could be made on the massive stones by turning them once they were placed on these points.

After the position of the stone within the monument was carefully marked, a hole was dug. The depth of the individual holes varied according to the length of the stones. Taller stones had deeper holes. Shorter stones had shallower holes. This ensured that the tops would all be level.

Three sides of each hole were vertical. The fourth side was at a forty-five-degree angle. The side opposite the sloped side was lined with timbers to keep it from being gouged as the stone was slid in. The stone was tipped into the hole and slid down the ramped side. Strong ropes were attached to the stones, which were then pulled upright into the holes. Atkinson estimated that pulling one stone upright took two hundred people.

After the stone was in place, the hole was filled with whatever was handy. Old tools, rocks, bones, stone scraps, and dirt were packed into the holes to keep the stones standing. This packing was stamped down. The giant stones were then allowed to stand for several months to let them settle before any more work was done.

Clues to Stone Placement

The placing of the standing stones has been fairly easy for archaeologists to reconstruct because the builders of Stonehenge left many clues behind. Excavation of several of the holes of the stones has revealed how the holes were shaped and what the packing materials were.

But many questions remain as to how the huge lintel stones were raised. These lintels are the stones which seem to hang between the standing stones.

Many archaeologists agree that the lintels were most likely raised on a tower of logs. The lintel was first placed next to the standing stones it was to cap. Logs were placed next to it. The heavy lintel was levered onto this base of logs. One end of the stone was raised and more logs placed beneath. Then the other end was raised and logs placed under it. Slowly, log by log, the tower rose, lifting the lintel to the desired height.

Another possibility is that the lintels were raised on earthen ramps. This method was used to lift the stones for the pyramids in Egypt. This theory proposes that long ramps were built extending from the base of the two stones to be capped. The lintel was then dragged up the ramp until it could be put into its proper place.

There are two major arguments against this idea. The first is that building the necessary ramps would have been a monumental task. To move the amount of dirt required would have taken more workers than

Raising the lintels would have been a challenging job. A common technique at the time was to use a platform of logs. By adding one layer of logs at a time, the stone was raised until it reached the top of the stones upon which it would rest.

This photo shows the ways the stones were shaped to ease their joining. Some had a "boss," the knob sticking out of the top of the stone on the left. Others, like the fallen stone, had socket holes. This type of joint has effectively held the stones in place for centuries.

were needed to dig the entire ditch and bank circle around Stonehenge I. The second reason is that no evidence has ever been found of either the holes dug to provide the dirt or even the shapes of the massive ramps in the soil.

Stonehenge and the Pyramids

The effort needed to build Stonehenge has often been compared to the work needed to build the Great Pyramid of Cheops in Egypt. Both Stonehenge and the pyramid are marvels of the ancient world because they are so large and because they were built with primitive tools and techniques. The Great Pyramid, built in 2500 B.C., has over two million blocks of stone. The average stone weighed two-and-one-half tons; the heaviest weighed fifteen tons. The pyramid stood almost five hundred feet tall, covering thirteen acres. It is estimated that hundreds of thousands of slaves labored to build this pyramid which served as the tomb of only one person.

The building of Stonehenge took over three centuries with the labor of hundreds, maybe thousands of workers. While we many never know if these workers were slaves, it is most likely that they were not. Instead, these were probably people dedicated to the idea of building a lasting monument. Even so, Gerald Hawkins, an astronomer and mathematician, calculated that it took at least one and a half million days of labor to build Stonehenge.

Over many years and after much investigation, archaeologists have discovered where the stones of Stonehenge came from and how they were shaped and erected. They have pieced together ideas of who the people were who built Stonehenge and how they built it. But we still do not know why Stonehenge was built. This remains Stonehenge's greatest unsolved mystery.

Five

What Was the Purpose of Stonehenge?

After years of scientific study, Stonehenge has slowly revealed the answers to many of its riddles. Archaeological investigations have unearthed the picks and shovels used in digging the holes for the gigantic standing stones. The mauls used to shape the huge stones have been discovered. Geological surveys have located the source rock for the massive stones themselves. Experiments have shown how many workers would have been needed to build Stonehenge in each of its different phases.

All of these archaeological puzzle pieces have helped us better understand the people who built Stonehenge. Each new clue dug from the earth has shown how these determined people constructed Stonehenge with the simplest of tools. But only a few clues give us any ideas why Stonehenge was built.

Why Was Stonehenge Built?

In Chapter 2 we examined various legends about Stonehenge: Merlin's engines, Stonehenge as a war memorial, Stonehenge and the devil, and Stonehenge as a Druid temple. These legends and tales were

An aerial view of Stonehenge. The circular mound in the background is one of many burial mounds in the vicinity of Stonehenge. Note how the Avenue crosses the road and the Heel Stone stands beside it. (Since this photo was taken, the roads have been changed.)

created to explain Stonehenge to generations long past. No single legend completely explains all of the attributes of Stonehenge. Not one fully explains why so much time and effort was spent building a gigantic stone monument on a lonely windswept plain.

Yet even today the towering stones stand, challenging people to discover the answers. Somewhere hidden in the stones lies the answer to the greatest mystery of all: Why was Stonehenge built?

Stonehenge Decoded

Over the years most investigators and visitors have agreed that somehow Stonehenge was connected to celestial observations. The alignment of the entranceway and the Heel Stone toward sunrise of the solstice, for example, demonstrated an awareness of this yearly event. Knowledge of the cycle of the sun was important to ancient peoples, especially those who lived in northern climates such as Britain's, because they had no calendars. In many cases their lives depended upon knowing when to safely plant their crops to avoid destruction from frost. If they planted too early, a frost might kill the young plants. Too late and the harvest would be ruined by frost or snow. By pinpointing midsummer, these people could plant and harvest their crops with less danger from severe weather.

Ever since William Stukeley in 1740 first recognized the alignment of the main axis to the midsummer sunrise, investigators have tried to understand the connection between Stonehenge and the stars. Yet no one is certain just how the people of Stonehenge used this alignment. Was it just a huge pointer aimed at the spot where the midsummer sun would rise? Or was the alignment of the entrance with the fifty-six Aubrey Holes some sort of calendar? Did the ancient people of Salisbury Plain use Stonehenge to predict important sunrises and sunsets? Did they use the monument to predict eclipses? Did the arrangement of the stones have anything to do with the setting of the moon at the winter solstice? Or was there no real purpose to the arrangement of the stones other than as a ceremonial backdrop for human sacrifice?

In 1901 Sir Joseph Norman Lockyer attempted to date the building of Stonehenge using astronomy. Lockyer, Astronomer Royal, believed the builders of Stonehenge had intentionally oriented its axis to the point on the horizon at which the midsummer sun first appeared. Lockyer, using a series of calculations and measurements based upon this alignment, concluded that Stonehenge had been built between 1880 B.C. and 1480 B.C. As the later archaeological investigations of Hawley and Atkinson showed, Lockyer's dating was remarkably close to the actual building period.

Hawkins and Stonehenge

In the 1960s, astronomer Gerald Hawkins from the Harvard College Observatory, became interested in the alignment of the stones at Stonehenge. In his astronomy book *Splendor in the Sky*, Hawkins wrote, "Stonehenge probably was built to mark midsummer, for if the axis of the temple had been chosen at random, the possibility of selecting this point by accident would be less than one in five hundred. Now if the builders of Stonehenge had wished to simply mark the sunrise they needed no more than two stones. Yet hundreds of tons of volcanic rock were carved and placed in position. . . . Stonehenge is therefore much more than a whim of a few people. It must have been the focal point for ancient Britions. . . . The stone blocks are mute, but perhaps some day, by a chance discovery, we will learn their secrets."

With the 1965 publication of his now famous book *Stonehenge Decoded*, Hawkins opened many eyes to new possibilities about Stonehenge. *Stonehenge Decoded* shook the fundamental beliefs of many scientists by linking Stonehenge to the sky. Hawkins's statements created controversy among astronomers and archaeologists alike. Many new questions were raised.

Gerald S. Hawkins, the astronomer who caused a furor with his book *Stonehenge Decoded*.

Few had specific answers. Many of the questions generated new questions.

What were these new theories that Hawkins proposed that rocked the foundations of Stonehenge?

The Secrets of the Stones

Gerald Hawkins had worked near Stonehenge as a young man. He had occasionally visited the ruins, noting that the center of the monument lined up with the Heel Stone and pointed to the midsummer sunrise. This alignment had been written about numerous times. In it he saw nothing new.

In the summer of 1961 Hawkins and his wife went to Stonehenge to try to unlock its celestial secrets. They purposely visited Stonehenge one week before the solstice to avoid the crowds they knew would be there for the midsummer sunrise celebrations. Hawkins had calculated that although they were a week early, the sun would be off its midsummer position by only one-half of its diameter.

Hawkins carefully set up his cameras, sighting down the axis line and including the Sarsen archway and the Heel Stone. At precisely 4:30 a.m. he saw what he had been waiting for.

In *Stonehenge Decoded* Hawkins described this moment: "Then suddenly, in the band of brightness to the northeast, we saw it—the first red flash of sun, rising just over the tip of the heel stone! It was a tremendous experience. The camera's whirring was the only reminder that we were not in the Stone Age; we experienced primitive emotions of awe and wonder."

As Hawkins wandered among the stones that day, he began noticing things as an astronomer would. Up to this point, almost all of the theories about Stonehenge had been made by archaeologists or storytellers. Hawkins's expertise as an astronomer made him see alignments that no one else had made sense of before. He wrote, "I felt strongly that the sunrise line had

If the Stonehenge builders had only wanted to mark the progress of the sun, they could have done it with just two stones. Why, then, did they build the complex Stonehenge?

certainly been carefully planned, and that many other stones had also probably been laid out with alignment intended. Indeed, as I peered over and between the stones, I came to feel that *all* of them might have been placed according to some master plan; their relative positions seemed so carefully arranged.''

That day he made four important observations and raised four critical questions.

Four Observations

The first observation was about the awe-inspiring impact upon Stone Age people watching the full disc of the sun rise precisely over the Heel Stone. After all, such precise alignments were not common in prehistoric lives. If he, Hawkins, a twentieth-century scientist, had been struck by the wonder of this moment, how would this event have affected prehistoric people. ''Why had such an alignment been so well established?'' he questioned.

Hawkins's second insight was the narrowness between the gigantic pillars. He noticed that his view was restricted when he looked between the stones. He felt as though his field of observation was being tightly controlled, that his eyes were being forced to look for something on the horizon. ''What was I supposed to see?'' he wondered.

He felt this control of his sightlines when looking through the archways, too. It was as if the builders of Stonehenge were forcing him to look *for* something, to look *at* something. ''Why was such viewing important?'' he asked himself.

The height of the Heel Stone and another stone standing outside the circle next attracted Hawkin's attention. Both stones were of such a height that an average-sized person could look right across their tops in a line to the horizon. ''Why were these stones set so precisely?'' Hawkins wondered.

''Most of these questions, I felt, might somehow be answered by astronomy. Those precise alignments

Stonehenge at sunrise.

Gerald Hawkins felt that the pillars were purposely set to restrict the view—but what was he supposed to see?

and controlled vistas, so carefully directing the eye to nothing visible, might well have been sighting-lines for celestial events such as special rise or set points of those godlike forces of prehistory, the sun, moon, planets, and stars. Primitive men observed with apprehension the places where the great rulers of day and night entered and emerged from the dark earth. It would have been natural that the Stonehengers should mark those points by various means.''

Hawkins felt that the most obvious purpose of

Many authorities believe that Stonehenge was built to mark the summer solstice.

Stonehenge was as a calendar; a huge, important calendar, marking one major day in the year, the summer solstice.

He wrote, "If you were only a simple Stone Age man, you might regard yourself as fortunate if you could be sure of marking one special day every year, and you might well take great pains to mark it, because from such a known day you could reckon forward to the times for plantings and harvests, hunting, and other vital concerns for the whole year, until the day came

"Now we begin to understand why the builders of Stonehenge I dug holes at uniform intervals around a circle, and why they did not erect stones or posts in them. The holes were fixed reference points along the circle. . . . Moreover a marker moved by two holes each day completes a circle in 28 days, not much different from the period of 27.3 days of the Moon in its path across the sky."

Fred Hoyle, *On Stonehenge*

"At the heart of Hawkins' and Hoyle's claim lie the 56 Aubrey Holes. . . . Both men assumed that the holes were used for holding tallies or markers. The archeologists argue that this cannot possibly have been the case, if, as they believe, the holes were filled up soon after they had been dug; besides, what was found in them was mostly cremated bones, so if they were used for anything it must have been burials."

Lionel Casson, *Mysteries of the Past*

again and the cycle was complete. The Stonehenge builders had done that. Their axis pointed to the place of sunrise at midsummer. They had given themselves an accurate marker for midsummer day."

After reaching these conclusions, Hawkins then went one step further. "What if Stonehenge had other important alignments with the stars, moon, and planets?" he wondered.

Looking at all the possibilities, considering the millions of mathematical calculations necessary to find additional alignments, Hawkins felt defeated by the gigantic stones.

"It's no use wondering," he said to himself. "To answer these questions—to find if these alignments have any celestial significance—we need precise measurement and comparison, a great volume of trial-and-error work—much more work than I can find time to do."

Still the questions persisted. Hawkins could not leave them unanswered. Then he found the solution. He would take accurate measurements of Stonehenge, hundreds of them, feed them into a computer, and let the computer do the hard work. He would give the computer the information to solve the 27,060 possible alignments between the 165 stones and holes.

Stonehenge in the Computer Age

Hawkins and his colleagues took a chart showing all of the recognized positions of stones, holes, and mounds at Stonehenge. They drew lines through these markers to the center of Stonehenge or through archway midpoints. They then fed this information into the computer.

The computer's main job was to find out just where these lines, if extended, would hit the horizon. After these points had been established, it would then match these horizon points with any known celestial event such as the summer solstice.

Hawkins explained it this way: "It was as if they

[the computer programmers] told the machine to stand at each of the selected points, look across each of the other points to the horizon, and each time report what spot of the sky it saw.''

Surprising Results

The investigators were surprised at the results. Repeatedly, the computer gave alignments for the positions of the sun at the summer and winter solstices. This supported Hawkins's original theory that Stonehenge marked important sunrises and sunsets throughout the year.

But what surprised him most was that Stonehenge also seemed to mark significant risings and settings of the moon.

Hawkins then told the computer to pinpoint where the sun and moon rose and set in 1500 B.C. The results

Stonehenge has captured people's imaginations for centuries. This painting by eighteenth-century poet-artist William Blake illustrated his poem ''Jerusalem.''

were astonishing. Hawkins wrote, "There was no doubt. Those important and often-duplicated Stonehenge alignments were oriented to the sun and moon."

According to Hawkins's theory, Stonehenge was a gigantic celestial calendar.

Hawkins was still puzzled, however. Why build such a complicated calendar when only two stones are really necessary to mark sunrise or any other celestial event? Why go to all of the backbreaking work to quarry, move, shape, and set up these huge stones if a simpler way would have been easier and served just as well?

Hawkins gives these answers to his questions: Stonehenge's main function was as a calendar,

This drawing shows some of the important correlations Gerald Hawkins found. They confirmed his belief that Stonehenge is a complex astronomical computer.

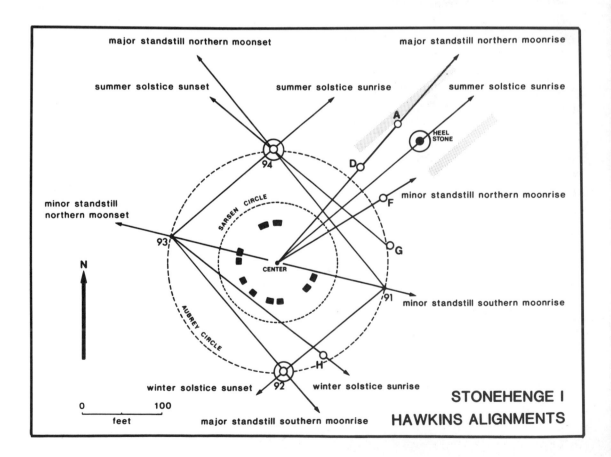

major standstill northern moonset

major standstill northern moonrise

summer solstice sunset

summer solstice sunrise

summer solstice sunrise

A

HEEL STONE

94

D

minor standstill northern moonrise

SARSEN CIRCLE

F

minor standstill northern moonset

93

G

CENTER

91

minor standstill southern moonrise

N

AUBREY CIRCLE

H

winter solstice sunset

92

winter solstice sunrise

STONEHENGE I
HAWKINS ALIGNMENTS

0   100

feet

major standstill southern moonrise

especially as a marker for knowing when to begin the planting season. Planting times were vital to early people. They had to know when to plant so as to avoid frost. One could not simply count backwards from warm days. It was easier and more reliable to pinpoint the rising of the summer sun, a predictable and repeated phenomenon.

Hawkins theorized that Stonehenge also served as a source of power for priests and their people. Imagine the power that priests would have over people when they could call them forth to witness the midsummer sunrise, events they alone could predict, he suggested. It is quite possible, Hawkins supposes, that these priests would be treated like gods.

Hawkins's third answer is that Stonehenge "served as an intellectual game." Why should these thinking, intelligent people stop with the simple alignments of Stonehenge I?

He answers his own question, writing, "I think that the men who designed its various parts, and perhaps even some of the men who helped build those parts, enjoyed the mental exercise above and beyond the call of duty. They had to set themselves more challenges, and try for more difficult, rewarding, and spectacular solutions, partly for the greater glory of God, but partly for the joy of man, the thinking animal."

Positive Response to Hawkins's Theories

Hawkins reported his findings in the British scientific journal *Nature* in 1963. The response was immediate. Newspapers around the world reported Hawkins's conclusions. The London *Times* wrote, "Professor Hawkins may not himself carry archaeologists the whole way with his arguments, but he has given them more to bite on than they have had before from any astronomer." A German paper ran headlines reading, "Puzzle of Stonehenge Solved." Articles, pictures, and poems appeared for months

"There can be no doubt that Stonehenge was an observatory; the impartial mathematics of probability and the celestial sphere are on my side."

Gerald S. Hawkins, *Stonehenge Decoded*

"If you toy with Stonehenge for long enough, you are sure to come up with something astronomical it can be made to do."

Archaeologist Christopher Chippindale, *Atlantic Monthly* magazine after. A comic strip artist even included Stonehenge in his comics.

Letters flowed in from around the world. Many people applauded Hawkins's work and his discoveries. Many others opposed his views and argued against his conclusions. Hawkins was surprised at the worldwide interest in understanding Stonehenge. One letter writer said, ''We are fascinated by your evidence of the amazing skill of those long-gone people.'' Another wrote, ''A student of myth learns early that religion and the calendar are the same thing in the young history of men and that temples were observatories and laboratories. Hence I was grateful for proof of the inevitable nature of Stonehenge.''

Hawkins's Theories Opposed

Not all of the responses were favorable. Many people questioned Hawkins's conclusions. Scientists, especially archaeologists like Professor Atkinson, were skeptical. Were Hawkins's measurements accurate? they asked. Had he placed more significance on some stones while ignoring others? Did Hawkins find what he set out to find, shaping his conclusions to support his theories?

Atkinson, the foremost Stonehenge archaeologist, called Hawkins's book ''arrogant, slipshod, and unconvincing.'' Atkinson detailed his arguments against Hawkins's conclusions in an article titled ''Moonshine on Stonehenge.'' Atkinson's major criticism was Hawkins's use of sightlines from only certain holes. These holes, according to Atkinson, were not dug by human hands but had been formed by tree roots. Atkinson also questioned Hawkins's emphasis on other sightlines which he felt were two degrees out of line. A two-degree difference does not seem like much, but it means the sightlines would entirely miss lining up with the moon. Atkinson also concluded that many of the sightlines calculated by the computer were chance alignments.

Archaeologist R.S. Newall, who had taken part in earlier excavations at Stonehenge and was the author of the official Stonehenge guidebook, questioned some of Hawkins's conclusions but supported some of his findings. He particularly agreed that the alignment of the stones pointed to the rising of the sun at the winter solstice.

Newall wrote to Hawkins saying, "It is always difficult, I suppose, when two different sciences meet, to come to an agreement. Astronomers have their eyes in the sky; archaeologists in the earth. However, I agree that Stonehenge is oriented to the winter solstice setting sun in the great central trilithon as seen from the center or anywhere else on the axis."

Newall also wrote, "I don't fancy it [the proposed astronomical function for Stonehenge] will be accepted by archaeologists until other sites that could have been used in a similar way are found in Britain or on the continent."

Hawkins had no disagreement with the archaeologists. In fact, he looked forward to their questions. Hawkins wrote, "Astronomy had established that there were many sun-moon alignments at Stonehenge—archaeology should seek to determine why."

Stonehenge as a Computer

Hawkins returned to the Stonehenge enigmas in 1964. This time he focused his energies on the alignments of the Aubrey Holes and reached another startling conclusion. Hawkins concluded that the Aubrey Holes were used to predict eclipses of the moon.

He theorized that the holes were a huge "Neolithic computer," suggesting that the priests of Stonehenge placed wooden markers in certain Aubrey Holes. By moving the markers, people could calculate and predict eclipses of the moon. Hawkins believed that a priest who could predict an eclipse would have great power indeed.

An aerial view of Stonehenge.

Hawkins reached this conclusion by noting that eclipses occur in a repeated cycle every 18.61 years. Three times 18.61, rounded off, is 56, the exact number of the Aubrey Holes. By moving markers from hole to hole around the ring, eclipses of the moon could be predicted.

Professor Atkinson immediately disputed this conclusion. Evidence from his archaeological digs showed that the holes had been filled up very soon after having been dug. Atkinson also pointed out that later building at Stonehenge destroyed many of the Aubrey Holes, leaving them useless for such astronomical observations.

Another famous British scientist, Fred Hoyle, professor of astronomy at Cambridge University, made his own analysis of the astronomical use of Stonehenge after examining Hawkins's sightlines. Hoyle agreed

A view of the trilithons.

that Stonehenge I was an astronomical instrument. But he disagreed with Hawkins's ideas about the huge standing stones of Stonehenge III. Hoyle believed that while these builders had great skill they did not have the astronomical knowledge to construct such a complicated celestial calendar.

Another major argument against Hawkins's theories is that he started with the idea that "If I can see such alignments, then the builders of Stonehenge must have seen them, too."

The problem with this hypothesis, opposing investigators argued, is that with so many possible alignments at Stonehenge, just about any event can be predicted, even the landing of men on the moon. Stonehenge can thus be used to predict Easter and Passover, two religious holidays unknown by the early builders of Stonehenge.

Obviously, there is some connection between Stonehenge and the heavens. What that connection is we cannot be exactly certain. Hawkins's theories seem to answer many questions about the astronomical significance of Stonehenge. Yet his theories also pose many more questions, questions that other investigators have not yet been able to answer.

Astronomer Fred Hoyle.

Conclusion

Will We Ever Solve All the Mysteries of Stonehenge?

Hundreds of books and articles have been written about Stonehenge. Almost every author has had some new ideas or theories about it. Some have seen new alignments in the great stones. Others have found mysterious markings on the stones which "explain" their purpose. Some have discovered ceremonial significance in the standing stones. Many more have studied Stonehenge from a scientific viewpoint, carefully researching and revealing the mysteries of the monument.

Over the years, some of the secrets of Stonehenge have been uncovered. Archaeological digs have told many things about the culture of the people who built Stonehenge. We know the tools they used, what they ate, and how they may have moved the gigantic stones and erected them. We know the stones do indeed have unique alignments with the sun and moon.

We can only guess, however, at how these alignments were used. We still can only speculate as to the ceremonies undergone in the shadows of the great stones. We can only theorize as to why Stonehenge was ever conceived and constructed.

The stones of Stonehenge still tower over Salisbury Plain. They stand as they have stood for thousands

Opposite page: Stonehenge, a place of mystery.

Will the mysteries of
Stonehenge ever be solved?

of years. Something in these huge stones speaks down through the ages to us in an ancient voice. The voice dares us to try to solve the mysteries of Stonehenge. We dig for evidence, we scan the skies for connections, we probe into the lives of the past for clues.

We may never know all the answers to the questions surrounding Stonehenge. Archaeological and astronomical investigations can carry us only so far back into the past. Unless we can somehow stand in the footsteps of the people of Stonehenge, we will never answer all of the riddles about it.

Still, the great silent stones challenge us to try to unravel their secrets.

For Further Exploration

Peter and Connie Roop particularly recommend the following books to readers who would like to learn more about Stonehenge.

R.J.C. Atkinson, *Stonehenge*. Hammondsworth, Eng: Penguin Books, 1979.

Peter Lancaster Brown, *Megaliths and Masterminds*. New York: Scribner's, 1979.

Lionel Casson, et al., *Mysteries of the Past*. New York: American Heritage Publishing Co., 1977.

Christopher Chippindale, *Stonehenge Complete*. Ithaca, NY: Cornell University Press, 1987.

Patrick Crampton, *Stonehenge of the Kings*. London: John Baker Publishers, 1967.

Geoffrey of Monmouth, *The History of the Kings of Britain*, transl. by Lewis Thorpe. Baltimore, MD: Penguin Books, 1966.

Evan Hadingham, *Circles and Standing Stones*. New York: Walker & Company, 1975.

Gerald S. Hawkins, in collaboration with John B. White, *Stonehenge Decoded*. New York: Double-day, 1965.

Fred Hoyle, *On Stonehenge*. San Francisco: W.H. Freeman & Co., 1977.

E.C. Krupp, *Echoes of the Ancient Skies*. New York: Harper & Row, 1983.

Euan MacKie, *The Megalith Builders*. Oxford, Eng: Phaidon Press, 1977.

Stuart Piggott, *The Druids*. New York: Thames & Hudson, 1985.

Colin Renfrew, *Before Civilization*. New York: Alfred J. Knopf, 1973.

Leon E. Stover and Bruce Kraig, *Stonehenge*. Chicago: Nelson-Hall, 1978.

Robert Wernick, *The Monument Builders*. New York: Time-Life Books, 1973.

Index

Picture Credits

About the Authors

Peter and Connie Roop majored in geology at Lawrence University in Appleton, Wisconsin. Peter, an elementary school teacher, writes historical articles and stories. In 1986, he was named Wisconsin Teacher of the Year. Connie, a junior high science teacher, serves as a science specialist for *Appraisal* magazine and writes for educational journals. They earned their Masters degrees in Boston and have taught in England.

The Roops have co-authored a dozen books for young people, including *Keep the Lights Burning, Abbie*, which was featured on public television's *Reading Rainbow*. They are the authors of four Great Mysteries: Opposing Viewpoints—*Dinosaurs, Poltergeists, The Solar System*, and *Stonehenge*.

Peter and Connie live in Appleton, Wisconsin, with their children Sterling and Heidi with whom they enjoy traveling, camping, and reading.